THE
*Five-Million-Dollar Gift*

# DYNASTY TRUSTS

*Why Leave Your Assets
Any Other Way?*

# THE
# *Five-Million-Dollar Gift*
# DYNASTY TRUSTS

## *Why Leave Your Assets Any Other Way?*

# SETH PEARSON · CFP™

Just Write Books
STAUNTON, VIRGINIA

Book interior design by Robert Mott & Associates, www.RobertMottDesigns.com

Printed in the United States of America.

ISBN: 978-0-9749830-7-3

*For my three children, Amy, Seth, and Michael:*
*I hope this will give you*
*the guidance you need to protect*
*your financial well-being*

# ACKNOWLEDGMENTS

S everal professionals were instrumental in preparing this book, helping to ensure its accuracy and timeliness. Kathleen Fowler, attorney at law, has given my clients many years of outstanding assistance with their estate planning needs, and her feedback during the writing of this book has been critical. Thank you, also, to all the members of our family office team, who support me every day.

# CONTENTS

# INTRODUCTION

Not long ago, *The Wall Street Journal* reported, "It's easy for the super rich to shield their fortunes from estate tax because they can afford savvy financial planners to set up trusts and other shelters."[1]

It's true the wealthy don't pay taxes like the rest of us; I know because I advise them. Yet it's not so much a matter of affording this kind of protection as it is of knowing you can have it. Not all of my clients are super rich, and it requires only five to ten hours of legal attention to implement a plan designed to eliminate estate taxation and maximize return.

In this book, I reveal how you can avail yourself of *The Five-Million-Dollar Gift* offered by the generation-skipping tax exemption provided in our nation's tax code. Any individual can leave up to $5.25 million tax-free to his or her heirs, but to benefit from this exemption, you need to establish the proper trust, one we call a *dynasty trust* (also sometimes referred to as a *legacy trust* and a *generation-skipping tax trust* or GSTT). Regardless of its name or initials, if it's drafted correctly, the trust's assets will be protected from a death tax,

---

[1] Shailagh Murray, "Permanent Repeal of Estate Tax Is Defeated in Senate Vote," *The Wall Street Journal* (June 13, 2002): page A4.

generation after generation, shielding your family and extending your gift over many lifetimes.

## How Trusts Can Help Anyone

As a Certified Financial Planner™ professional, my experience advising hundreds of families for more than three decades has led me to view all of our children (both yours and mine) in two very broad categories:

> **Trust Me: It's a Loophole.** A loophole is a legal opportunity to save tax. It may startle you to learn that in 1995, the Internal Revenue Service Joint Committee on taxation reported that 31.8 percent of estates valued at ten to twenty million dollars legally paid no tax whatsoever. How did they do it? The following list includes many of the loopholes used by the wealthy to avoid estate taxes: *dynasty trust, family partnership, qualified personal residence trust, credit shelter trust, grantor-retained annuity trust, sale to defective grantor trust, Christofani trust, family foundation, charitable lead trust, charitable remainder trust, wealth replacement trust,* and *Crummey trust.* These trusts not only reduce or eliminate taxes, but they also avoid capital gains taxes, bypass probate, and enhance charitable deductions. But only the dynasty trust—the subject of this book—can provide tax avoidance, family access, asset protection, and total control for generation after generation.

+ Those who are hard working but need help with things like educating their children and affording their own retirement.
+ Those who create significant wealth and income in their own right.

The dynasty trust will help people in both of these profiles. The hard-working, middle-class children like mine will probably inherit their parents' estates when they are in their mid-fifties. Because my wife and I have a trust, it will provide the funds to pay off our grandchildren's student loans and ultimately create a stream of income in our descendents' retirement years. Not only will it supplement and enhance our children's finances, but it will also, I hope, remind them of how much their parents cared for them, and how seriously we worked and saved.

I feel strongly about the extended legacy of the trust. My wife and I would like to leave a lasting impression after we're gone. Proper allocation of the ten-million-dollar generation-skipping tax exemption when we die is like pouring the plaster in which we'll leave that enduring imprint.

By the time my children inherit the dynasty trust their mother and I have established, we will have had plenty of opportunities to discuss how it works, who the team members are, and why they have been selected. By then, I hope, our children will have addressed their own needs, including their children's education and their own retirement, but the inheritance should be a substantial gift, enhancing their well-being and supplementing their own savings. The plan, then, is not to restrict the beneficiaries in any way, but to add a level of value that, on their own, they would be unable to duplicate.

Primarily, I've written this book for my clients, their families, and my family. I hope to encourage all of them to get to know the dynasty trust, help them become confident in its unsurpassed ability to keep hard-earned wealth in the family for generations, and provide peace of mind that the money is being handled in their best interests. If you want to establish or maintain a dynasty trust for your family, then *The Five-Million-Dollar Gift* is for you.

Think how important your dynasty trust could be in your children's lifetimes. It will preserve their inheritance, avoid estate taxes, and even provide them with income and a legacy they can pass on to their own children. Why leave assets any other way?

# PART ONE:

## The Five-Million-Dollar Gift

*"No matter who you are, making informed decisions about what to do with your money will help build a more stable financial future for you and your family."*

—ALAN GREENSPAN

# Keep Five Million Dollars Tax-Free (Ten Million If You're Married)

Living trusts are needed in every basic estate plan. They serve multiple purposes, including avoiding probate, minimizing death taxes, and directing how the assets will be distributed. Probate is the court-supervised administration of your assets before they can pass to your heirs, and it is expensive. Probate means loss of complete control, takes on average eighteen months, and is unnecessary. (Note: Taxes and probate are unrelated.) Probate is created by your will, and putting assets in a living trust avoids probate. Probate property includes all property in an individual's name, or as a tenant-in-common, or joint tenants after the second spouse dies, or property payable to the estate when one dies.

It's easy to avoid probate.

Most people think they have avoided probate when they have a trust. Yet assets have to be placed inside the trust in your lifetime to avoid the state court administration requirement.

The federal government has nothing to do with the state probate process of administering an estate at death. The overall cost of probate can range from two to twelve percent of the value of the gross estate, while the national average is around six percent. Most of these expenses are paid to the attorney and the bank executor if there is one. The interests of these professionals are generally not in alignment with the family's, because the bigger the estate, the bigger the estate tax, the more complicated the probate—the more money the professional makes.

That may explain why most people who have trusts have not avoided probate. Their advisors have not completed the estate plan. They didn't put probate assets in the trust. Probably the reason probate costs so much is that it takes so long (average eighteen months). Probate is also public, so anyone can see what the value of the assets are, where they are, who got what. It is a source of information for many unscrupulous thieves who prey on innocent beneficiaries.

Why would any family want probate? If you have probate assets in two or more states, such as real estate you own in both Florida and Massachusetts, you can expect two probates and most likely two attorneys. It's simple to avoid probate, and it should be the number-one goal of every estate plan.

Once that goal has been achieved, the next recommendation is to establish a family bank that will begin when the first spouse dies. A family bank is a trust designed to create a pool of wealth that can benefit a family through multiple generations without diminution at each generational level by the normal wealth transfer taxes. The trust is referred to as a family bank because, like a bank, the trust is a prime resource for funding the particular needs of various beneficiaries in successive generations. The family bank is often referred to as a dynasty trust. One of the principal planning elements of a family bank, the dynasty trust, is avoidance of tax.

In the United States, you live under one of two tax systems. It could be the one for Those Who Plan, which rewards you for your foresight. Or it could be the one for Those Who Don't Plan, which takes advantage of your lack of knowledge or preparation (or both).

Under the tax system for Those Who Plan, you can pass on a little more than $5.25 million dollars per spouse to your family—without taxes—if you know about and use something called the *credit shelter generation-skipping tax exemption*. During your lifetime, you can prepare for this by setting up a dynasty trust, so-named because it looks after your family and your financial interests, both today and in the future.

In this book, you'll learn all about dynasty trusts, why they are so valuable (even if you don't have five million dollars), and how you and your family can benefit. You'll see how you can protect your assets and their appreciation from both lawsuits and transfer taxation, and how your family will retain access to and control over your money, for ninety-nine years after your passing—or longer.

**dy•nas•ty :** 1 : a succession of rulers of the same line of descent  2 : a group of individuals having power or authority in some sphere of activity and being able to choose their successors  3 : a family that establishes and maintains a predominance in a particular field of endeavor for generations

The dynasty trust creates a family bank that can benefit your family through multiple generations without reduction by normal death taxes. This family bank is a prime resource for funding the particular needs of the beneficiaries in successive generations. The family bank is also referred to as a GST-exempt trust.

## Use It or Lose It

If you don't use this exemption, you lose it when your assets pass to the next generation. In other words, unless you open the trust in your lifetime, this five-million-dollar gift goes away forever. And that's not all you lose. Your family stands to lose fifty percent of the value of your assets every time ownership transfers to the next generation. So it's not only when your children inherit that you lose fifty percent, but every time their children do, and so on, until your legacy has been whittled away within a few generations.

This is the cost of ignorance and inaction. With what you learn in this book, you can help your family not only avoid those estate taxes, but also increase the value of your assets, and do so for as long as they follow the plan you've created for them, for as long as your dynasty trust stays in force— quite possibly forever.

---

**The Tax Is Back.** The U.S. government levies estate taxes at death when assets change ownership through inheritance. Congress originally instituted it in 1797 to pay for wars, and it has been abolished three times: in 1802, 1870, and 1902. Then, in 1916, Congress brought it back yet again, and it has remained in force ever since. Recent administrations have tried to abolish it once more, but it is safe to assume that even if it does go away for a time, it will inevitably return to tax the uninformed. Why not retain control over some or all of your assets the informed way? Why not protect and preserve your wealth from the greedy estate tax?

---

## How the Rich Get Richer

In the early 1900s, financial giant and presidential papa Joe Kennedy set up a dynasty trust to hold one of the largest office buildings in Chicago. Less than a hundred years later, the building sold for more than five hundred million dollars, even more than the Kennedy patriarch might ever have imagined. Since the building was held in trust, this asset escaped taxation for three generations—while paying income to the beneficiaries. Assuming the family keeps the proceeds from the sale in the trust, that money will remain completely shielded from the legal liabilities that continue to plague Kennedy family members. (No matter who gets charged with what, or who divorces whom, that money in the trust is locked up for family use only, and no one, not even the law, can take it away.)

In the 1980s, wine makers Ernest and Julio Gallo protected more than $208 million by establishing their own trust. Before 1989, the tax law allowed for an unlimited amount to be placed in trust, so most multimillionaires took full advantage of the amazing tax savings and legal security offered by doing this. For the United States Congress, who were well-aware of how much money was *not* being paid to Uncle Sam by the super-rich, the Gallos' gigantic trust was the last straw, so the law was changed to allow for a maximum of $2 million per person. The new maximum is now $5.25 million per person, indexed for inflation.

Of course, old trusts are still in force, and no matter how the law changes now, the assets these families had the foresight to protect in trust remain untouchable. And though today's allowable amount would not cover the great fortunes of the Kennedys and the Gallos, $5.25 million tax-free in a dynasty trust can still make a huge impact on the legacy you leave to your family.

## You Don't Need a Million To Benefit

While you may not have the millions of these moguls, you can still make a significant contribution to your family by insulating your assets from creditors and transfer taxes forever. Add up the value of your house, your investments, your life insurance, as well as any other key possessions, and the total is probably significant.

Consider this hypothetical example, starring Clark and Janet Gable. This couple, who have together raised two children, run and retired from a small law practice, and diligently saved and invested, established a dynasty trust in their early seventies. Into the trust, they placed their $400,000 house, $100,000 life insurance policy, and $500,000 held in bank accounts and invested in mutual funds, stocks, and bonds. To their children's sorrow, both of them die in their eighties, leaving a total of one million dollars in the dynasty trust.

After their death, the parents' heirs (who are both in their fifties), watch the trust grow in value and enjoy the benefits of being paid an income from it. Let's assume the total return was eight percent (five percent for the income and three percent for the principal growth). In this case, the heirs would receive $2,055,000 of income over the next thirty years. During that time, the trust would grow to be worth $2,427,000.

The entire time Clark and Janet were alive and held their assets in the trust, and for as long as the family keeps the trust in force and doesn't withdraw the assets, the family enjoys the maximum protection from the potential liability of divorce or bankruptcy, as well as the certain liability of certain state estate taxes. They have also been able to receive

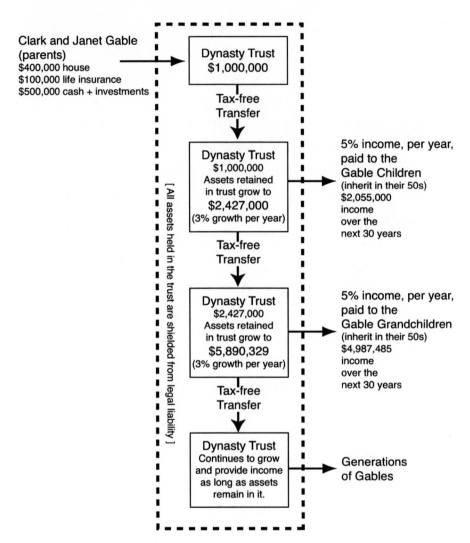

income from the trust, even to borrow from this "family bank" if need be, and to retain complete control over the family's money.

Throughout the rest of this book, you will see how you, too, can create security for your assets during your lifetime while extending that protection in perpetuity—to cover the wealth of your family for as long as the trust is alive, generation after generation. One gentleman characterized the dynasty trust as "the glue that keeps the family together." In addition to the advantages you've already learned, you'll see how the trust can also provide family privacy and confidentiality, sustain family values, and help those family members not trained in the investment, legal, or accounting fields.

Even if your children decide to spend all of the assets in the trust, at least the principal is protected from liability until they draw it all out. There is no better way to leave whatever you have to your children.

Mr. and Mrs. Jones are a hypothetical family who wish to take advantage of the new tax law that allows them to put $10.5 million in two Dynasty Trusts.

Mr. and Mrs. Jones, both age seventy, use the exemption and set up the trusts naming each other as beneficiary and trustee. Five years later, at age seventy-five, Mr. Jones predeceases his wife. Now Mrs. Jones is the beneficiary of his $1 million IRA account that was not in the trust. Mrs. Jones is also the settlor or creator of the directed trust she set up for her husband. As the settlor, she will control and direct how the funds are invested in this $5.25 million trust. As the beneficiary of the $1 million IRA account, she will have total control of that asset, and she is the trustee and beneficiary of the other $5.25 million Dynasty Trust set up for her benefit. Mrs. Jones can manage all of the assets during her lifetime or hire and fire financial advisors, at any time, if help is needed.

Assuming a 6 percent rate of return before taxes, Mrs. Jones could draw 8 percent from the $5.25 million Dynasty Trust and the $1 million IRA account for the next twenty-four years. That is $480,000 a year until age ninety-nine when she dies.

The three children then inherit the Directed Dynasty Trust she originally set up for her husband. It grew at 6 percent over the twenty-four years, from $5.25 million to $20 million. All of the growth in the trust ($15 million) passes tax-free to the children, saving $6 million based on existing federal tax law.

The three children divide the assets in three Dynasty Trusts for each family. This inheritance is now protected from liability and taxation in perpetuity just like Joe Kennedy's Dynasty Trust. The children are the trustees, and they now have absolute control over how these funds are invested and distributed.

According to *The Wall Street Journal* in January 2011, "Congress has set sweet new terms for the gift tax, and families are tearing up their estate plans to take advantage." This is truly a window of opportunity and an opportunity of a lifetime for families like the Joneses.

What are the costs to establish the trust that saved the hypothetical Jones family over $6 million? The answer here, where I work, is about $6,000 depending on the time it takes to customize the documents for each family's unique circumstances. Since the family is acting as trustees, settlors and beneficiaries, they control everything including the fees they pay their advisors. Because the family knows that no one cares more about their money than they do, they will always retain the right to hire and fire their advisors, accountants and lawyers.

# Summary

At 6 percent, the estate grew from $11 million to $20 million over Mr. and Mrs. Jones' lifetimes. Mrs. Jones drew $480,000 a year from the investments for twenty-four years after her husband predeceased her. After taxes, she had more than enough to cover all of her expenses and to make gifts to children and grandchildren as needed. The family maintained the maximum control possible while saving over $6 million in death taxes. The trusts provide asset protection from most forms of liability including: divorcing spouses, professional liability and automobile liability.

Dynasty Trusts can benefit every family, not just the wealthy. The idea is to protect inheritances from creditors and "predators" as well as save state and federal death taxes for many generations.

According to the February 2011 edition of *Trusts & Estates,*

> *" . . . there are multiple benefits to making such gifts despite the potential for recapture. First, the post-gift income and appreciation on the gifted asset escape estate tax (and recapture). Second, if the gift is made to a grantor trust, the grantor's payment of income tax reduces the estate and thus benefits the trust. Third, if GST tax exemption is allocated to the trust, it remains GST tax-exempt. If the donor doesn't use the $5.25 million GST tax exemption and it's decreased at his death, his opportunity to use it is lost. Finally, donees have the use of the gifted funds."*

If there is recapture, Mrs. Jones would be advised to spend down the $5.25 million trust she originally gifted while letting the other trust grow, achieving the same $6 million federal estate tax savings.

The February 7, 2011 Fortune magazine reported:

*"Indeed, the amount of money you can now transfer tax-free to your heirs if you do so while you are alive—as opposed to bequeathing it to them at death—is stagering. Daniel L. Kesten, an attorney at Davis & Gilbert in New York City, says that a couple in their fifties could put $10 million into a type of trust that would allow them to pay the taxes on the gains during their lifetime and, by doing so, move more money out of their estate. He calculated a scenario for a client who lived for 30 years after setting up what's known as an 'intentional defective grantor trust' and paid the taxes the whole time: If the assets grow at 5 percent, the heir would receive more than $43 million free of estate taxes.*

*Bergman has clients who have basically done that. The couple had already put $2 million into a trust for their only son, using up the previous gift-tax exemption. In January they put another $8 million in trust, and they plan to pay the income taxes over the next two or three decades of their lives. (This gift exemption is separate from the annual gift exclusion. Under current rules, anyone can still give $14,000 a year to as many people as he wants without having to pay a tax.)*

*Leiha Macauley, an attorney at Day Pitney in Boston, added that giving money while you're living also reduces the amount that will be subject to additional taxes at the state level. Currently twenty sates have estate taxes—with rates up to 16 percent—whereas only one has a separate gift tax."*

Urgent attention should be paid to state gift taxes. Now, states like Massachusetts are calculating how much revenue they will lose because of the federal gift tax changes. In my example of the Jones family $10 million transfer, Massachusetts loses $925,000. At any time Massachusetts could simply add gift taxes. Acting now before these potential changes could save the family almost $1 million.

Because no one cares more about your estate than you do, it is wise to explore all the options you have to save taxes.

# 2 | *Retain Complete Control*

**M**any commercial banks today provide a special service called "private banking" to their wealthier clients. It offers all the usual: car loans, house mortgages, and so on, plus help for its clients to decide what financial vehicles or products are best for their families. For anyone who establishes a dynasty trust, which can be called a *family bank*, it can function as a private bank. It has all the perks of regular banking, plus a few more.

With the family bank, while you are alive, all of your assets remain available only to you. You can still spend it all or give it away. When you die, part or all of your estate is left in the dynasty trust, and thereafter, your beneficiaries can own assets in the family bank, and they can borrow from it without jeopardizing any of the assets. They can also put their own assets in the family bank and reap all the benefits of the dynasty trust for their own possessions. Furthermore, money to pay for all expenses, such as food, schooling, education, clothing, and so on, can come from the family bank. The family retains complete control of all the funds

# FAMILY BANK

## SERVICES

### YOU RECEIVE:

Personal Trusts

Access to Experienced
Attorneys
Financial Planners
Accountants

Mortgage Lending

Checking/Debit Cards

Education for
Inheritors of Wealth

Consolidated Statements

Financial Opportunities
Screening

Family Control

Estate and Income Tax
Reduction

Concentrated Stock
Diversification

Asset Allocation

Asset Preservation
and Enhancement

## CUSTODY

### IT HOLDS:

Stocks

Bonds

Real Estate

Family
Limited
Partnerships

Family
Businesses

Airplanes

Commercial
Real Estate

Living Trusts

Crummey Trusts

Family
Foundations

Charitable
Lead Trusts

Charitable Trusts

and decides when and whether to use the money for themselves. The goal, of course, is to leave as much in the trust as possible so it is protected, but if family members' income or investments aren't sufficient to pay personal expenses, they can elect to distribute principal and draw income as needed.

---

**Terms of the Trust.** The world of trusts is filled with language that may be unfamiliar to you. Here's a review of the most common words associated with dynasty trusts.

The person who creates the trust is the *creator, settlor, grantor,* or *donor*. The assets in the trust are the *corpus, trust res, trust fund,* or *trust estate*, which is separate from any income earned by it. The *trustee* is the person who holds title to the property in the trust for the benefit of another person, called the *beneficiary*. The legal agreement that establishes the trust and details the duties and limits of the trustee is the *trust indenture*.

---

# The Ultimate Investment in Your Family

In the example of the previous chapter, the Gable Family Bank, which was originally funded with one million dollars in assets, provided an average of more than sixty-eight thousand dollars a year to the Gable children over thirty years, and that amount increased for future generations. In addition, the Gable family had a rising principal in the trust against which they could take interest-free and tax-free loans. Just thirty years after the Gable children inherited their parents' million-dollar gift, it had grown to $2,427,000 — more than twice the original amount.

Let's say the Gables' daughter, Bonnie, owns a home worth $250,000, and she also has a son getting ready to go to college. Rather than take a second mortgage based on her home equity (which could be much less than $250,000) to help pay for tuition and housing, Bonnie could simply place her house in the trust and withdraw an amount equal to its value. *The $250,000 would be hers to spend as she saw fit without ever paying interest on it or ever repaying the money she's received.* She could also continue to live in the house for as long as she wished, and if she had been paying a mortgage, the trust would assume the payments. It would also pay the property insurance and any expenses associated with upkeep. Furthermore, it would completely protect the house from any sort of legal liability. Even if Bonnie didn't have a son on his way to college, she might be wise to put her house in the trust.

If Bonnie didn't have a house to put in the trust, she could still opt to take the cash out of the trust, either as an interest-free and tax-free loan, or as a straight withdrawal that would never have to be paid back into the trust. Bonnie has many options for funding her son's education, and the complete freedom to choose whichever one best suits her situation.

22

Consider what your family could do if this kind of money were available to them through a family bank! Perhaps it would mean less stress, an incentive to invest rather than just pay the bills each month, better education for future generations, even improved health care and more fulfilling retirement. Establishing a dynasty trust is an unequivocally sound investment in your family and its future.

## All's Fair

Suppose Bonnie's brother, Hank, didn't have an asset of equal value with related expenses to put in the trust. To be sure both of them would benefit equally, they could decide that Bonnie should lease her house from the Gable Family Bank, and her rent payments would therefore offset the disbursements for the mortgage, insurance, and so on. The trust value would not decrease in any way as a result of her transaction.

Alternately, if the Gable parents had foreseen that Hank and Bonnie would want the money handled differently (if, for example, Hank would want to withdraw his share while Bonnie wanted to keep hers in trust), they could have decided to fund two separate trusts for their children.

There are myriad ways to ensure that all beneficiaries receive exactly what the creators of the trust intend; these are just two examples. Your dynasty trust is a flexible, accommodating instrument of your desires for your family. All you have to do is express those desires, and the trust fulfills them.

# Your Family's Financial Office

Of course, a trust is not a magic wand; creating it, monitoring its value, and maintaining it require experts who are trustworthy in both senses of the word. In addition to the family bank, select advisory practices provide clients with a *family financial office* staffed with skilled estate planning attorneys, financial planners, and tax accountants. Although they are not the subject of this book, other kinds of trusts are available from such a financial office to help clients minimize personal income taxes, sell a business without capital gains tax, and so on. The purpose of the family financial office is to provide ongoing, comprehensive care to the client and client's family for anything affecting their financial lives. A family office is available to answer any question at all related to money.

One of the most significant benefits of this financial office is the continuity it provides to the family. After the death of the trust's creators, their estate continues to be handled as they wished, by the same folks who helped them establish the trust in the first place. The family gains an education, even before inheritance if they want it, on any and all matters of their own personal finance. They are brought up to speed on all aspects of the dynasty trust so that, once they assume control of it, they fully understand their role and responsibilities, as well as the resources available to them through the family financial office. This is perhaps the best possible way to preserve the wealth created in one generation and enhance it for future generations.

**Finding Financial Help.** Every day, family offices help people decide on things like the best way to pay for their children's education, the best mortgage strategies, long-term care options including assisted-living properties, and real estate sales and purchases. They screen investment alternatives and offer income tax reduction strategies. It is a privilege to help multiple generations with their unique financial concerns.

In the U.S., there are probably a thousand family offices, which are able to deliver this level of service. It's important to develop a relationship with one of them as soon as possible so your family has time to evaluate the team and build trust. As mentioned earlier, when you find the right advisors, you will save much more money than it will ever cost. Consider these questions as you evaluate whether it's time to build your own family office now:

*Do you receive meaningful information from your accountant, attorney, and investment advisor now?*

*Is the reporting integrated and timely?*

*Do you know what your advisors are doing to help you?*

*Do you receive information to help you make important financial decisions?*

*Are you paying too much for investment services?*

*Are you confident that all your administrative needs are being met?*

*Are you spending too much time on financial matters and not enough on family matters?*

25

*Will your spouse know what to do when you die?*
*Will your existing will and trust really do what you want?*
*Are your children ready to manage their inheritance?*
*Are you wealthy enough to meet your needs in all situations?*
*Are your attorney, accountant, and investment advisor*
*working together to help you achieve your goals?* ⇒

Below is a list of the services provided by firms as part of the family financial office. With a little research, you could build a coordinated team anywhere to meet all your wealth management needs, teach you what you don't know, and help you apply what you learn.

# Financial Office Services

* Reduce or eliminate transfer (estate) taxes and capital gains taxes
* Provide superior investment administration with continuous supervision and management
* Increase the family's long-term wealth
* Maintain absolute confidentiality
* Implement financial and estate plans
* Provide one consolidated statement for all family brokerage accounts and hold brokers accountable for performance and commissions
* Minimize all expenses and fees
* Provide financial education to the inheritors of wealth

- Develop financial assets and earning capabilities of younger family members
- Protect assets from liability, litigation, and probate
- Screen financial opportunities presented to family members
- Care for family members who have special needs
- Unburden inheritors from responsibilities external to their particular family and career
- Help the family maintain complete and absolute control over assets
- Help the family achieve a sense of significance and satisfaction derived from how assets are used
- Consolidate and simplify an efficient, fully integrated wealth-management process
- Access experienced attorneys, accountants, and financial planners
- Search the world for the right services and products at the lowest possible cost
- Establish intergenerational financial continuity using cutting-edge technology and innovation

## Summary

The hypothetical Jones family from chapter 1 would take these steps to maximize family control. The parents would be trustees of each other's Dynasty Trust. When one spouse died, the surviving spouse would continue as trustee of one trust and as the settlor of the other trust, and would control how it is invested. Congress has set new terms ($5 million) for funding Dynasty Trusts, and families are tearing up their estate plans to take advantage. Tax laws will come and go to cover deficits, but the tax-free status of the Dynasty Trust can go on forever.

In the next chapter, you'll learn more about where to set up your trust, read some guidelines and caveats for selecting a trustee and staffing a "financial office" to oversee the family bank, and see how you can avoid conflicts of interest. You'll learn solutions that put absolute control over the family bank in family members' hands, assure intergenerational financial continuity, and foster a family profit center. You'll be ready to create a fully integrated wealth-management process. Why leave your assets any other way?

# 3  Make the Right Choices for the Long Term

Y ou now know you must establish your trust in your lifetime to ensure that you are able to make this multi-million-dollar, tax-free gift to your family. But how soon should you do it? Perhaps you are still feeling youthful and energetic and know you'll be around for quite some time. Maybe you come from a long line of centenarians, and you are planning to blow out those hundred candles with your great-grandkids when the big day arrives. If that's so, congratulations and best wishes for your continued good health, but please also accept a bit of advice: No matter what your age, the time to establish your trust is now.

A person of forty with significant assets has just as much reason to establish a dynasty trust as does someone who is eighty. Shielding assets from legal liability, and providing a way to appreciate those assets to a much greater amount (while still meeting the requirements of the generation-skipping tax exemption) benefits you and your family no matter how old or young you are. It should go without saying that, as capricious as life can be, its end is often even less predictable, but it's still a point worth making. Scare tactics won't get you to establish your trust today, but what good is there in waiting? The key to any wealth transfer plan is to begin during your lifetime—the sooner the better. Remember, if you don't use it, you lose it.

Even if you don't expect your assets to grow beyond the allowable exemption in your lifetime, you can still use the dynasty trust while you're alive to make your assets lawsuit-proof and estate tax–free forever. Once your assets are in the "vault" of your dynasty trust, they are literally untouchable, except by you. Moreover, even if you establish the trust now, it doesn't have to be funded until after your death. You can hold all your assets for as long as you like and transfer ownership to the trust only when you are ready. There is literally no downside to acting sooner rather than later.

When you are ready to move forward with your dynasty trust, there are two key decisions that will impact its ability to maximize benefits to your family. You must choose a trustee, foreseeing and preventing conflicts of interest, and determine in which state your trust will be established. The rest of this chapter will help you evaluate each of your options so you can make the best choices for yourself and your family, both now and in the future.

# Choosing Your Trustee

When you create a trust, you name a trustee, the person who will hold title to the property for your beneficiaries after you die. The responsibilities of the trustee are to carry out your instructions, hold trust assets in secure custody, handle accounting and tax returns, administer the trust and keep records, and communicate with the beneficiaries. Selecting the trustee is key to the long-term success of your family's trust.

Basically, you have four choices: your children, someone else you know, a local bank, or an independent trustee in partnership with your financial advisors. All of these choices have advantages and disadvantages, so let's review each of them in turn.

*Your Children.* Many people opt to name their children as co-trustees of their trust. If the Gables had set up their trust this way, both Bonnie and Hank would have had the power to make a complete distribution of their respective shares of the trust. If Hank did not withdraw all of the funds in his lifetime, the remainder would continue to benefit his children in the same way; likewise for Bonnie. Of course, both Hank and Bonnie could elect to withdraw all assets, and the Gables' grandchildren would receive no benefits of the trust whatsoever.

Having children as co-trustees allows the family to invest in stocks, bonds, or real estate without a trustee fee.

*Someone You Know.* No doubt you could save some money, again on fees, by naming someone you know—a friend, relative, or advisor—as trustee. Yet you have to ask yourself if these people have the time, the skill, and the financial savvy to manage and administer your trust. Heaven forbid they take on the job and think they do when they don't.

Even if they do take your interests to heart and want your trust to be handled expertly, wouldn't they have to hire people to help them, thereby defeating the cost savings you might have wanted for your family? What's more, when you establish a dynasty trust, you create a structure to provide long-term benefits for generations. Certainly, no family friend or other individual will survive the terms of the trust. In fact, you'd hope your trust outlives anyone you know by many, many years.

***Your Local Bank and Trust.*** The first question you must ask yourself when considering the local bank and trust as trustee is whether your state offers the best environment for investing, tax reduction and, most important, distribution. Your bank, obviously, will be bound by the laws of its state, so this is an important factor.

You must also consider the likely longevity of your bank. In the late 1990s and on into the early 2000s, more than six thousand banks disappeared from the scene as a result of mergers and failures. At the end of 2002, *The Wall Street Journal* reported, "Horror stories abound of banks that make beneficiaries practically beg for their own money, trust officers who won't return phone calls, beneficiaries stuck with toll-free numbers to nowhere, and assets being steered to financial institutions' poorly performing proprietary mutual funds."[2] The article recommends a web site, www.heirs.net, to gather more information on these problems.

Bank consolidation has led to the unhappiness of many families and a wave of lawsuits accusing corporate trustees of mismanagement and putting their own interests ahead of their customers. The Jones family has been dealing with this for many years. Granite Trust Company, which funded their

---

**Be Careful Who You Trust(ee).** William Averell Harriman inherited a railroad fortune in Union Pacific. Free to pursue his well-financed political interests, he was the ambassador to the USSR and Great Britain, and he held the distinguished positions of U.S. Secretary of Commerce and governor of New York. He even made a bid for the Democratic presidential nomination in 1956.

In 1986, he died, leaving the bulk of his $100 million estate in trusts. He had chosen two close friends to act as co-trustees, Clark Clifford and Paul Warnke, who invested the money in real estate deals—and lost an estimated $41 million, nearly half the estate. At this writing, the family is suing the trustees in the hopes of recouping some of what was lost.

*(Continued on next page.)*

---

[2] Kelly Greene, Ruth Simon, and Anne Marie Chaker, "Trust-Fund Kids Get Assertive in a Down Market," *The Wall Street Journal* (December 17, 2002): page D1.

*(Continued from previous page.)*

Were Clifford and Warnke ill-equipped? You wouldn't have guessed it. Clifford was an advisor to Harry S. Truman, foreign policy advisor to John F. Kennedy, and chairman of the Foreign Intelligence Advisory Board supervising all U.S. espionage operations. He was Secretary of Defense in Lyndon Johnson's cabinet and went on to become a wealthy corporate lawyer. He died in 1998, and now the Harriman family is suing his estate. (For Clifford's family's sake, you have to hope he left his assets in a dynasty trust.)

Not short on brains either, Warnke was the head of the Arms Control and Disarmament Agency and Jimmy Carter's chief negotiator in the Strategic Arms Limitation Talks with the Soviets.

No matter how qualified your advisors seem to be, the family must retain control. Your family can't delegate away the supervision of the assets, or they could lose everything. ➵

trusts, was taken over by South Shore Bank and all the relationships changed. Then South Shore was taken over by Multi-Bank, who maintained almost 100 percent of the trust assets in

their own stock. When that bank was taken over, the Jones family was told the trust money wasn't theirs when they complained about poor performance. Then Bank of Boston was taken over by Fleet Bank with a whole new regime of indifference, and most recently Bank of American took over Fleet.

The Jones' children's generation will ultimately have access to the principal, but so much aggravation could have been avoided if the trusts had allowed the family to hire and fire the trustees as needed. This is the solution: From the very beginning, retain the ability to remove the trustee and replace him or her with someone else. This must be a part of the original trust documents, and you must insist on this. Most boilerplate trust documents won't allow for it because change does not benefit the trustee in any way. Instead, it's in your best interest. Be sure you check your documents!

***The Independent Trustee in Partnership With Your Financial Advisors.*** One of the key incentives to hiring a team of trust professionals is that pros are accountable for their errors. If your children or a family friend were to make a mistake with your trust's assets, it would be a shame, but they would not be held legally responsible.

Perhaps more important, though, the professionals can have the expertise, the experience, and the impartiality to help your family make the best possible choices for the trust. Of course, experts must be compensated for their assistance, and fees for trust services vary. Fees should be disclosed from the beginning, so you and your family know exactly what will be paid. (For more on appropriate fees, see the next chapter.)

# Preventing Conflicts of Interest

No matter whom you choose as your trustee, it's vital you and your family explicitly retain the right to replace the trustee with whomever else you choose. Yet you won't find this kind of flexibility in the typical bank trust document. Just ask for a sample to see for yourself that the bank is most interested in protecting its interests, rather than yours.

Of course, the problem is conflict of interest and hidden agendas. Typically, when a family is at the office of a financial advisor for the first time, they arrive with a fragmented plan. The attorney has written a will. (Sometimes there's a trust, but most of the time there are no assets in the trust.) As you now know, if the will were to be used at death,

---

**Nice Work If You Can Get It.** William Donaldson, the head of the Securities and Exchange Commission, was once trustee of the $350 million Ford estate and charged a fee of $1 million a year. The primary beneficiary, Kathleen DuRoss Ford, asked a judge to bar Donaldson from collecting this outrageous fee for what was described by other attorneys as "no work." Donaldson finally settled and took $1 million for the first year, $550,000 for the second and third years, and then agreed to resign.

In choosing your family's trustee, be aware of the usual fees for this service, and don't accept exorbitant charges. Fees should be disclosed and competitive.

---

it would create probate. Attorneys are needed for the probate process, and in the end make much, much more money probating the estate than they did when they initially drafted the will or trust. So there is the attorney's conflict of interest.

James White was reading his will and trust before signing it. When he saw the attorney's fee for probate, he was startled. It was three percent of his estate, which amounted to more than $2 million in attorney's fees. To the lawyer's credit, this fee was disclosed, but the client found it to be exorbitant, so he didn't sign the will. Soon after, he retained a financial advisor to help him establish his own family bank to avoid probate and outrageous fees.

If you are talking with your local bank and trust company about becoming your trustee, beware of possible conflicts of interest there, too. The bank may want you to set up a credit shelter trust naming them trustee and becoming irrevocable after you die. They may also ask you to name them as executor. In this case, the hidden agenda is to charge fees for managing money and settling the estate. Without proper drafting, the family can't fire them even if they charge too much, perform poorly, or fail to provide adequate service. Many respected institutions do not meet their fiduciary duty to their clients, so be sure you address this up front.

Individuals can also have conflicts of interest. I heard one frightening story of a retirement community, populated mostly by the elderly rich, where a well-regarded old banker was often named trustee for trusts with real estate in them. As trust manager, he had the grantor give him power of attorney.

Upon the death of a landowner, the banker would hold an unpublicized auction to which he invited only a select group of friends and relatives. Someone would purchase the real estate at a ridiculously low price, perhaps twenty percent of its real value. The grantor's family members would be told the house sold under-market for some concocted reason, the trust would receive the proceeds, and at some time in the not-too-distant future, the banker's cronies would sell the real estate for the going rate and reap a handsome profit.

Wherever there are humans, there is the possibility of conflict of interest. Wealth just compounds the problem. So you must seek tested, trusted, caring advisors who will work on your behalf, not theirs. Watch out for hidden agendas and hidden costs. Look for a coordinated team of experts who disclose all fees and are intent on making a comprehensive plan that works for you, not them.

The illustrations starting on the next page show how two different models of financial planning operate. The first is the fragmented approach with the family's resources being drained out in multiple directions to support a variety of agendas.

# COMPETING AGENDAS

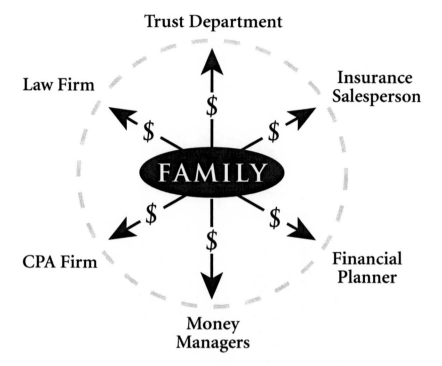

Certain problems with this are obvious: There are multiple conflicts of interest, hidden costs, and no doubt a hodgepodge of uncoordinated investments, insurance, and estate "planning," if you could call it that.

Next you see the family bank model with all the services operating together and toward the aims of the family.

This model offers a fully integrated wealth management process, absolute family control, intergenerational financial continuity, and a profit center for the family.

# COORDINATED FAMILY FINANCIAL OFFICE

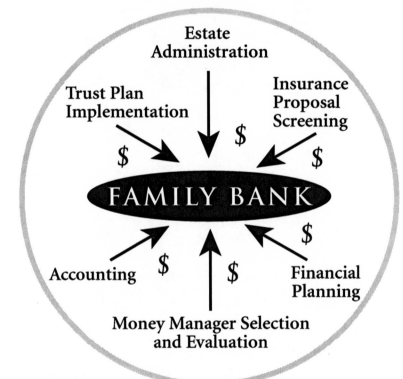

A Registered Investment Advisor works for you. A broker works for his firm. The conflicts of interest are exemplified by the last Great Recession and the unprecedented deficit it left us with. Influenced by greed, thousands of Wall Street brokers perpetrated the largest fraud in world history, leading to the stock market crash of 2008–2009. Watching fellow brokers achieve sudden wealth, status and power, many took even bigger risks with investors' money to fuel their own jealous, irrational, flawed, human avarice. What is amazing to me is that not one broker has served one day in jail for this $1 trillion fraud.

What should we learn from these all-too-human conflicts of interest? For one thing, it happened before and it will happen again. I ask you why you should pay *someone else* to gamble with *your money*? You can't control a broker's lust for more than he needs or deserves. But you can control how your money is invested, by simply using Modern Portfolio Theory and low-cost, passive index funds.

Recently, Vanguard passed Fidelity to become the largest mutual fund company. One of the main drivers of Vanguard's growth is the Registered Investment Advisors' fiduciary responsibility to put the interests of their clients ahead of their own. Because the advisor does better when the client does better, the biggest conflict of interest is removed. As more advisors embrace this passive strategy, more investors are protected from the middlemen. The Nobel Prize winning philosophy is "a penny saved, is a penny earned". Vanguard index funds cost 5 times less than the average cost of actively managed stock funds.

Your best defense against conflict of interest is two-pronged: 1) insist upon the right to remove and replace the trustee at any time, and 2) ensure that all financial matters are coordinated through a family bank. The first is simple: just keep your eyes open and be clear with anyone drawing up your paperwork. The second is also simple, except that it may take some research to find the right firm for you.

## Decide How to Put Your Assets In the Trust

Everyone should use a simple, revocable trust to avoid probate. All assets subject to probate should be put into the trust now. However, you have complete freedom to choose when and how you fund your dynasty trust. You could opt to set up the trust but keep it "empty" until your death, at which time, all the assets you want to leave to your children would be transferred to the trust. This would make a lot of sense for a couple with assets that won't exceed the exemption and who have sufficient insurance coverage to protect the assets from liability during their lifetime.

The main benefit of funding a trust while you're alive is to gain the asset protection, so if this is not a concern, it could be more cost-effective to hold off on the transfer of ownership until later because there can be fees associated with administering the trust once it's funded.

You could also opt to put some of your assets in trust and add as you go, or put everything in as soon as the trust is established, to consolidate your assets and really take advantage of all the perks of the family bank. It's entirely in your control.

**Protect Your Home.** Families with significant equity in their homes may want to place a residence in the dynasty trust sooner rather than later. As mentioned before, this allows the family to place a valuable asset in trust that could appreciate to an amount that would exceed the exemption—but it will still be covered by the exemption as long as it's put in trust before its value exceeds $5 million per person. It also provides the maximum protection possible from liability.

Likewise, a few people may want to keep the family compound or vacation home in the family for future generations. The dynasty trust is ideal for this type of planning. Assets in the trust will be transferred tax-free, generation after generation, with the maximum protection from liability possible. But as with all assets, it is important to give your beneficiaries clear instructions to avoid conflict. Three families owning a vacation house together could easily create just the kind of friction you want to avoid. (Remember, you can change the independent trustee any time you want, but make sure the replacement doesn't charge you an investment fee on the residential real estate in the trust.)

Later, your children can buy their own homes inside the trust. For example, if John Jones leaves $1 million of his estate when he dies to a dynasty trust, and the money is invested in liquid assets like stocks and bonds, each of his three children could invest $330,000 of that money in their own primary or vacation residence. This scenario is far superior to taking the money out of the trust and then buying the property.

## Summary

Of course, no book written about secure investing today can ignore the threat of a Madoff type of scam. If the family retains complete control, they can demand that investments are custodied with a safe and insured custodian like TD Ameritrade, Vanguard, Fidelity or Schwab. They would hire only advisors that must, by law, put the family's interest ahead of their own. They would never deposit funds to the advisor's account, only to the insured custodian. They would receive statements monthly from the custodian and not from the advisor.

The next chapter will help acquaint you with costs for trust services, compare fees to the value actually provided, and outline a sample trust so you can see how the process and the strategy work together.

# PART TWO:

# Making The Most Of Your Dynasty Trust

*"I find the great thing in this world is not so much where we stand, as in what direction we are moving; to reach the port of heaven, we must sail sometimes with the wind and sometimes against it— but we must sail, and not drift, nor lie at anchor."*

—OLIVER WENDELL HOLMES

# *See the Whole Financial Picture*

If you're still reading at this point, you're at least intrigued by what a dynasty trust could do for your family. You realize it will keep your estate from being chopped in half when your children inherit it, and again when their children inherit it, and so on. You understand how it will help your descendents build the kind of wealth they probably could not create on their own. And you plainly see that putting assets in a dynasty trust provides maximum asset protection from liability.

You're probably also wondering what such a trust will cost. Be reassured that the advantages of a trust will, in almost every case, create a net gain for the family, not a net cost. You do, however, need to be mindful of appropriate pricing as you seek to find the right agency to handle your trust.

The kind of trust you're reading about is dynamic, flexible—and affordable. This trust has only a modest cost, which, in many firms, is offset by volume discounts with the nation's major money managers and passed on to clients, the avoidance of attorney's fees for probate, and the elimination of estate taxes. Fees related to taxable securities are also deductible for most people. Estate settlement costs are significantly reduced because of the simplicity of administration and the continuity inherent in the dynasty trust.

When you establish a trust, you should receive the following services:

- safekeeping of assets,
- investing based on the family's instructions,
- distributing income and/or principal to the beneficiaries,
- filing all personal and business tax returns,
- issuing monthly statements, and
- ongoing availability to your family to help with any money-related concerns or questions.

What does it actually cost for a firm to administer your dynasty trust? It depends on the size of the estate, but here's an example just so you have an idea. If you were to establish a million-dollar trust with half in tax-free bonds and half in index funds, the total fee for the investment advisors, the tax return, and all the services mentioned above could be 0.5% per year , or $5,000 for the first year. That's much less than the average cost of a mutual fund for the same size investment.

Of course, the initial meetings should incur no fees and no obligation. And simply setting up the trust has a cost, usually about three thousand dollars. It will be five to ten hours of legal fees, and if you choose not to fund the trust until after your death, there is no administration cost. (However, the benefits of funding the trust—of putting your assets under its protection—in your lifetime can be substantial, as you are now aware.) In some cases where individuals are using the trust only to avoid probate fees and estate taxes, and they have sufficient insurance to cover any potential liability, putting off funding until death makes the most sense.

You have many ways to maximize your investment and minimize fees, depending on your needs and situation. Cost, then, is no reason to avoid the trust. Saving money, on the other hand, is the reason to embrace it.

The rest of this book provides you with specific strategies for your own dynasty trust, including how to select a financial advisor, steer investment choices for your assets, and guide your children to learn all they can so that, when the time comes, they are ready to take the helm of your family's dynasty trust.

# Choose the Best Financial Advisor For Your Family

Companies that care about the continuity they can provide for clients' families plan for their own future, too. They set it up so service can continue undisturbed by the death or disability of any particular individual; in other words, if the president were to be hit by that proverbial bus tomorrow, the financial firm's clients would not be adversely affected.

How can they do this? By having multiple owners and succession plans in place that ensure uninterrupted continuity of service. They also have licensed professionals in their twenties, thirties, forties, and fifties at the firm. New, younger professionals will be trained and, with the experience of time, step up to more responsible roles inside the financial headquarters.

In time, the people will change, but your firm's goals should remain constant. A trustworthy financial firm is a valuable company, one that encourages team professionals to grow and improve it over the long term. They are experienced at providing financial services for families all over the country, no matter where the beneficiaries may live.

The following is offered as a reference guide to selecting a financial advisory firm for your family.

# Mission

A good family office has the following mission statement or one like it:

+ We are independent. We work for our clients and not a corporate parent.
+ With our clients, big or small, every dollar counts.
+ When our clients succeed, we succeed.
+ Our client's best interests and our own are one and the same.
+ We offer the most competitive combination of services and investment alternatives available anywhere.
+ We expect our partners to work as hard for us as we do for our clients.
+ We improve the lives of those we serve.

When you are selecting the financial firm for your family, ask for their mission statement. (If they don't have one, move on.) In the financial planning industry, Bob Veres is a Ralph Nader–like advocate who is known and respected across the nation. Recently, he published a list of mission statements he liked, some of which are included here to give you an idea of what you should expect from the best advisors:

+ "Providing the clarity and confidence you need to make successful financial decisions."

* "We are committed to providing timely, unbiased advice to people from all walks of life. Through advantages of professional, fee-only planning, we seek to empower our clients to make the best financial choices possible. As a staunch consumer advocate and fee-only client fiduciary, we continue to demonstrate our dedication to serving the public's best interests. Whether you are just setting out on your financial journey, or seeking to protect and enjoy the wealth you've accumulated, we can help you along the way."

* "We will build lifelong relationships with our clients, and the friends and family they refer to us, through prompt, professional service, and honest, understandable advice. We will endeavor to earn the trust they place in us by always keeping their objectives ahead of our own."

* "The mission of our practice is to provide the highest quality of service, expertise, and integrity in a timely manner so our clients can better their lives financially."

* "We believe the best interest of our client must be first and foremost in all of our decisions, but the ultimate welfare of our clients and that of our firm are inseparable."

* "To serve as a trusted advisor who helps people make smart choices about money. To help clients make the best possible financial decisions, those that lead to peace of mind and build financial independence."

- ✦ "Operate in a way that makes it easy for clients to use our services, to understand their own and our individual roles and responsibilities, to experience consistently responsive service and to feel comfortable expressing their needs and opinions."

- ✦ "Our mission is to provide financial peace of mind for individuals and families by advising them with time-tested, common sense, tax-efficient and risk-controlled approaches to wealth accumulation, management, and preservation in a personalized and cost-effective manner."

- ✦ "Our purpose is to give you honest and understandable advice of the highest quality; helping you to be financially secure, so you can maintain and improve the quality of your life."

Behind each of these mission statements are financial advisors who can provide the services required to make your dynasty trust a profit center for the family and not a financial drag on performance. Ultimately, the team should provide clarity and peace to your family's financial life. Your advisors should be caring team players with integrity and accountability at the core of the relationship. The trust you put in them is their greatest reward, and their objective advice should facilitate good financial decisions for future generations.

Your team should be big enough to offer the universe of services and small enough to give you the personal service you deserve. It's not the size of the account that drives good firms. It's the success they are able to help their clients achieve that is the best measure.

# Compensation

Remember, the level of compensation your team receives should be directly linked to the performance of the portfolio. The accounting and legal professionals should be paid by the hour at competitive, reasonable rates. The best advisors have credentials; an important one is Certified Financial Planner. And no matter how good or experienced your professional help may be, you have to stay involved. You cannot delegate away this responsibility or ultimately you will lose a great deal, if not all, of the assets.

The staff of a multiple family office would consist of a team like mine:

Certified Financial Planner™ professionals
Family Office Accounts Manager
Operations Manager
Registered Service Associates
Accounting Specialists
Estate Planning Attorneys
Legal Assistants
Certified Public Accountants
Certified Financial Analysts

# Qualifications and Questions to Ask

We suggest you get to know a team of professionals now, before your family really needs them. Meet with as many firms as necessary until you feel comfortable and confident that a long-term relationship will be successful.

For a firm to be worthy of your consideration, it should be providing seamless financial solutions, not selling products. It should be committed to your family's multiple generations, both now and in the future. It should have a formalized succession plan in place so the continuity of service is not jeopardized by the death or illness of a team member.

Your team should have years of hands-on experience with integrated financial strategies such as:

+ Retirement Plans
+ Gifting
+ Generation-Skipping Trusts
+ Charitable Remainder Unitrusts
+ Charitable Lead Trusts
+ Qualified Personal Residence Trusts
+ Crummey Trusts and Trusts for Minors
+ Executors and Trustees
+ Intentionally Defective Trusts
+ Living Revocable Trusts
+ Asset Protection Strategies
+ Self-Canceling Installment Notes
+ Founder Stock Issues
+ Strategic Asset Allocation

- Marital Trusts
- Qualified Domestic Trusts
- Tactical Asset Allocation
- Family Limited Partnerships
- Grantor Retained Annuity Trusts
- Private Foundations
- Donor Advised Funds
- Gift Annuities and Pooled Income Funds
- Irrevocable Insurance Trusts
- Restricted Stock and Stock Option Issues
- Charitable Remainder Trusts
- Hedging Strategies
- Optimized Portfolio for Taxable Investors

As you begin your search, ask about other clients of the firm in which you are interested. Are they like you? Typical clients for many advisers are retired, in their sixties, with two or three children. They have been married for forty years or more and are in good health. Individually, they are vastly different and include families whose wealth was acquired through medicine, industry, real estate, and other professional services.

The firm you want to choose communicates with its clients in ways that educate the *entire* family and support sound decision-making. Frequently, firms send newsletters to their clients. As you are checking out a firm, ask for old issues. What was the firm saying to its clients when the stock market was at its peak in the beginning of 2000, and what is it telling its clients now? Look for realistic assessments, useful information, and a lack of hyperbole. For example, you are looking for a newsletter that alerts clients about overpricing in the market when it is outrageously high (doesn't get them all excited about buying more, more, more), and also encourages people to expect the inevitable rebound when the market is at its worst (doesn't spread doomsday predictions). The advisor should be offering a steady hand and counteracting media overreactions and propaganda.

In the end, the firm you choose should take you to your destination with a feeling of safety and confidence throughout the journey. If not, don't hesitate to look for a better fit. You truly can centralize the family's financial affairs under one roof.

## Finding the Right One

Financial advisory firms exist to provide financial counseling. There are more than 750,000 brokers, insurance agents, and advisors in the United States, with 300,000 of them offering services as financial advisors. About forty thousand are Certified Financial Planner™ professionals. But an elite cadre of advisors exists. These professionals are serious about maintaining their independence from the typical institutional conflicts. Frequently, they serve clients all over the country. If you're having trouble finding them, keep looking: They're out there. Ask friends and family for referrals, and don't settle for anything less than exactly what you're looking for.

After a few meetings with potential advisors, you should receive a simple, comprehensive written plan to help you make intelligent decisions. You should feel comfortable that you were provided the information you need to lead your financial advisors. And you should feel a new sense of security about your financial affairs. This is the minimum you should expect from the very beginning of the relationship.

# 6

# *Strategically Invest Your Trust's Assets*

**M**ost advisors you trust today won't be here when the time comes to administer your trust's assets for you children and their heirs. What road map can your family and their advisors follow to achieve maximum income and growth with as little risk as possible?

It's been said that change is the only constant. That's certainly true, so we need the best system to deal with future challenges. Modern portfolio theory is the cornerstone of my recommendations. Two people who won the Nobel Prize for economics are considered the founding fathers of this sophisticated investment-decision approach, which allows an investor to classify, estimate, and control both the kind and the amount of expected risk and return. If it's good enough for Bill Gates, Warren Buffet, Vanguard, Fidelity, State Street, and all the other major financial institutions, then it certainly is good enough for your family.

The history of modem portfolio theory reads like the story of the invention of the atomic bomb, with years and years of research by the best and brightest thinkers in the world leading to a conclusion that changed the world forever. Modern portfolio theory is the cornerstone of making investment decisions today.

Long-term investors need stock because these investments have provided the best hedge against inflation for more than seventy-five years. Portfolios need stocks to provide income for life.

But what is the best way to invest in stocks? The University of Chicago's Harry Markowitz, Ph.D., earned the 1990 Nobel Prize for his work that originated in 1952 and laid the foundation for modem portfolio theory. He proved that "if two portfolios have the same average return, the one with the lower volatility will have the greater compound rate of return over time."

In a nutshell, when you put this theory into practice, diversification reduces volatility, which enhances performance. Consider this example:

|                        | Investment A | Investment B | Investment C |
|------------------------|:------------:|:------------:|:------------:|
| Year 1 Return          | 8%           | 8%           | 8%           |
| Year 2 Return          | 6%           | 0%           | –6%          |
| Year 3 Return          | 10%          | 16%          | 22%          |
| Simple Average Return  | 8%           | 8%           | 8%           |
| Compound Annual Return | 7.99%        | 7.8%         | 7.39%        |
| Volatility             | Low          | Medium       | High         |

See how, in column A, the low volatility results in a better return overall: With the yearly return fluctuating at most four percent each year, the compound annual return is 7.99 percent. And although the *average* return is the same for all three investments (eight percent), as the return swings more wildly, the critical number—that compound annual return— falls in columns B and C.

Although it's clear, the above example gives you an understated effect of volatility. Now let's look at it in real life. Since 1926, the S&P 500 Index (roughly speaking, this includes the biggest five hundred companies in the U.S., weighted by their capitalization) lost forty-three percent in its worst year. If only half was in stocks, then your loss was only half as much. Over the long term, diversification—and thus the reduction in volatility—enhances returns. It's simple math.

William F. Sharpe, Professor Emeritus, Stanford University Graduate School of Business, shared the 1990 Nobel Prize in economic sciences with Harry Markowitz, the university

professor whose work is mentioned above. His math proved
that the stock market portfolio consisting of all stocks had
the least volatility, which is how we define risk. These two
academic discoveries led to a breakthrough in investment
methodology, which, we now know as modem portfolio
theory. In other words, they proved that less risk (volatility)
led to the highest rate of return. Isn't that what everyone
strives for?

In 1973, Burton G. Malkiel, professor of economics at
Princeton University, published *A Random Walk Down Wall
Street*, adding more proof to the theory that owning all stocks
is the most efficient way to reduce risk and enhance returns.

All of this research did not go unnoticed. John Bogle
(following his graduation, magna cum laude, from Princeton
University with a degree in economics) went on to create the
first index mutual fund and in 1975 founded Vanguard, the
largest nonprofit money manager in the nation. The index
fund gives you all the stocks (Bill Sharpe's hypothesis), which
has led to the lowest volatility and highest return (Harry
Markowitz's Nobel Prize-winning theory). Past performnce is,
of course, no guarantee as to future returns.

The academic research and industry collaboration led to
the "atomic bomb" of investing: the index fund. Index funds
consist of stocks or a representation of stocks that exist in an
index like the total U.S. stock market index. The fund simply
holds those stocks. On average, the professionals who
actively buy and sell those stocks to try to add more value
end up underperforming the index fund. Most respected

academics agree that the reason the pros underperform is because of their expenses.

If the index solution produces the highest return on average with the least amount of risk (volatility) then investing for a lifetime of income is very simple. Most academics are in agreement as the following article excerpts point out:

### The Man Your Fund Manager Hates

Burton Malkiel has been saying since 1973 that professional money managers can't beat the market. Today his words are accepted wisdom. . . . Few investment calls have been so right for so long as the one that Burton Malkiel made twenty-six years ago. In his book, *A Random Walk Down Wall Street*, Malkiel made the case, originally posited by the University of Chicago's Eugene Fama and other academics, that it is futile to try to pick winning stocks. The market, he wrote, is efficient: It so rapidly gathers information and incorporates it into stock prices that it's impossible for even the smartest investors to outguess the market consistently. The only strategy that makes sense is to invest in an index fund, one that blindly tries to reproduce—but not beat—the market's return.("The Man Your Fund Manager Hates," *Fortune*, December 10, 1999, page 135)

### The Case for Index Funds

Perhaps the biggest advantage of indexing for the taxable investor lies in its tax advantage of deferring the realization of capital gains or avoiding them completely if the shares are later bequeathed. . . . I am convinced that most investors—both individual and institutional—will find the guarantee of playing the stock-market game at par every round a very attractive one. . . . As Nobel laureate in economics Paul Samuelson states, "Investors would be well advised to avoid looking for such tiny needles in such large haystacks." The chances of identifying the very few managers who will beat the market are close to nil. (Burton G.

67

Malkiel, "The Case for Index Funds," *Mutual Funds*, February 1999, page 75)

## The Best Way to Own Common Stocks

Most investors, both institutional and individual, will find that the best way to own common stocks is through an index fund that charges minimal fees. Those following this path are sure to beat the net results (after fees and expenses) delivered by the great majority of investment professionals. (Warren Buffet, Berkshire Hathaway Incorporated, 1996 annual report)

## Can't-Miss Moves to Make Now

Buy an index fund. Last year, passively managed funds once again beat the returns of the majority of actively managed funds, according to Morningstar. Index funds guarantee you the market's rate of return, plus the benefits of low costs and tax efficiency. ("Can't-Miss Moves to Make Now," *Money*, March 2002, page 63)

## Index Funds Outperform More than
## Seventy-Five Percent of Actively Managed Funds

Most actively managed funds are destined to trail the performance of index funds. The logic is simple. Index funds earn the market return. Before taking into account costs, actively managed funds as a group must also earn the market return because together they are the market. But costs (operating expenses, management fees, and brokerage commissions that are expressed as a percentage of a fund's assets) are typically 1.5 to 2 percentage points greater for actively managed funds than for index funds. Most active managers simply don't have the stock-picking skills to overcome that cost differential. . . .

Studies consistently show that index funds outperform more than seventy-five percent of actively managed funds over almost any reasonably long time period, such as five years or more. The index-fund advantage is even greater if failed actively managed funds—those that have closed or been merged out of existence—

are included. In addition, there is no reliable way to predict which funds will outperform the market. (Alfred Rappaport, "Shareholder Scoreboard (A Special Report): The Best & Worst Performers of the WSJ 1000; Before You Start: Questions You Should Ask Yourself About Investing in Stocks," *The Wall Street Journal*, February 28, 2005, page R8)

## Strategies for Investors Who No Longer Believe That Anyone Can Really Predict Which Mutual Funds Will Beat the Market

Fewer than twenty percent of all equity funds outperformed the unmanaged S&P 500 index in the past year. The percentage drops to eleven percent over ten years and to four percent over a fifteen-year stretch. And despite the solemn import that fund companies attribute to past performance, there's no evidence that the four percent who beat the index owe their record to anything other than random statistical variation. (Bethany McLean, "Strategies for Investors Who No Longer Believe That Anyone Can Really Predict Which Mutual Funds Will Beat the Market," *Fortune*, March 15, 1999, page 129)

## Can We Still Rely on Index Funds?

Yes. The case for matching the market—instead of trying to beat it—is as strong as ever. (Jason Zweig, "Can We Still Rely on Index Funds?" *Money*, September 2002, page 104)

## Over Ten Years, Most Active Funds Underperform Their Benchmarks
*Administrative costs cut into returns, study finds*

Actively managed mutual Funds consistently underperform their benchmark indexes by about three to one, a new study shows. The study, which tracks ten years of mutual fund performance, was done by Fulcrum Financial, a division of Fulcrum Financial Inquiry LLP in Los Angeles.

According to the study, fund investors in every size category do not make out as well as they would by investing in the related market index. Eighty-one percent of value funds underperformed, along with seventy-two percent of blend funds and sixty-three percent of growth funds.

The main reason for the underperformance was administration costs, which cut into total returns, according to David Nolte, one of Fulcrum's founders.

They included management fees, sales load/redemption fees, brokerage fees and spread costs. "These things are so difficult to overcome," he said. (Jennifer Blecher, "Over Ten Years, Most Active Funds Underperform Their Benchmarks," *Investment News,* December 6, 2004)

### Exxon Mobil Goes Passive in a Big Way
*Merged funds abandoning active management in 2003*

Exxon Mobil Corp's $14 billion 401(k) plans are dumping active investment management.

The company, formed through the merger of Exxon Corp. and Mobil Corp. in 1999, will go to an almost one hundred percent indexed format when it merges the predecessor plans in mid-2003. ... "We're really not trying to take away anything, but give Mobile employees a better deal because we believe the index funds, on average, will outperform active funds because of fees," the Exxon Mobil official [Kathy Taylor] said. (Vineeta Anand, "Exxon Mobil Goes Passive in a Big Way," *Pensions & Investments,* September 16, 2002, page 1)

### Husbanding that $27 Billion
*Harvard's Jack Meyer doesn't see future returns matching past yields*

Harvard Management CEO Jack R. Meyer made outsize returns on the $27 billion he invests for the university. Recently he gave a rare interview to William C. Symonds, Business Week's Boston bureau chief. Here are excerpts: . . .

**How can individual investors find managers who can beat the Street?**

Most people think they can find managers who can outperform, but most people are wrong. I will say that eighty-five percent to ninety percent of managers fail to match their performance benchmarks.

**That's pretty pessimistic.**

Yes. But because mangers have fees and incur transaction costs, you know that in the aggregate they are deleting value. The investment business is a giant scam: It deletes billions of dollars every year in transaction costs and fees.

**What should individuals do?**

Most people would simply have index funds so they can keep their fees low and their taxes down. No doubt about it. (*BusinessWeek*, December 27, 2004, page 119)

## Best Predictor of Future Returns

Research shows low cost rather than past performance is the best predictor of future returns. (*Wall Street Journal*, November 18, 2012)

The academics, regulatory agencies and most professionals agree: when it comes to investing, past performance has zero predictive value. (*New York Times*, January 6, 2013)

Best predictor of strong mutual fund performance is low fund fees according to research at Morningstar Inc., Chicago, which tracks 360,000 investment offerings. (*Bottom Line*, October 1, 2010

"Since trading costs cut into returns, they are a powerful predictor of negative performance according to a study conducted by Roger Edelen of Boston College and Richard Evans of University of Virginia. (*Investment News*, July 9, 2007)

A study updated last year of thousands of US stock funds put the average trading costs at 1.44% of total assets. Expenses are one of the most important things investors can look at. (*Wall Street Journal*, March 3, 2010)

Nearly all actively managed US equity mutual funds underperformed their benchmarks (Indexes) in the 12 months ended June 30, 2012, a particularly extreme example of the typical outcome in the ongoing debate between active and passive investing, according to a report Standard & Poor's releases twice a year. (*Journal of Indexes*, January/February 2013)

Investors are jumping out of mutual funds managed by professional stock pickers and shifting massive amounts of money into lower-cost funds that echo the broader market (Index funds). It also reflects that many money managers of stock funds, which charge fees but also dangle the prospect of higher returns, have underperformed the benchmark stock indexes. (*Wall Street Journal*, January 4, 2013)

The Center for Retirement Research at Boston College supports the concept of moving to lower fee structures. In a paper released last month, the organization's director, Alicia H. Munnell, proposed banning high-fee actively managed mutual funds from 401(k)s and rollover IRAs. "Virtually all researchers agree that most actively managed equity funds can be expected to underperform index funds once fees are considered," she wrote. "It makes no sense to expose the average participant to these options." (*InvestmentNews*, April 1, 2013)

## Down With Mutual Funds?

Who is David Swensen and why should you pay attention to him? He's one of the most successful money managers in America today. In twenty years of running Yale University's endowment, he has outdone his peers, by far. His returns have averaged 16.1 percent a year. . . .

Swensen has a single recommendation: Opt out of the mutual-fund merry-go-round. He sits on the board of TIAA, whose TIAA-CREF mutual funds he admires for "low costs and investor orientation." But he recommends Vanguard for its even lower costs and selection of index funds.

For long-term investors managing money in tax-deferred retirement accounts, he suggests something like this: 30 percent in U.S. stocks (a Total Market index fund, for both large and small stocks); 20 percent in international stocks (a Total International index fund); 20 percent in real-estate stocks; 15 percent in U.S. Treasury bonds (for protection against financial crises), and 15 percent in Treasury Inflation Protected Securities—Treasury bonds whose interest rate rises and falls with the inflation rate. You'll find similar funds at Fidelity Investments and T. Rowe Price. This [is] not only investing made easy, it's investing made smart. (Jane Bryant Quinn, "Down with Mutual Funds?" *Newsweek*, Aug. 29/Sept. 5, 2005, page 45)

## Like Them or Not, We Need Mutual Funds

Two of America's premier investors have written new books with a common message: The mutual fund industry is bad for your financial health.

David Swensen, the author of Unconventional Success, has managed Yale's endowment for two decades, during which time he has earned better returns than anyone—including his counterparts at Harvard. John Bogle, whose book is called *The Battle for the Soul of Capitalism*, is the founder of Vanguard Investments, which manages more long-term mutual fund money than anyone—including Fidelity.

Bogle has long been a critic of his industry. Swensen is new to the field, but he writes about mutual funds with language the muckrakers once used to describe the meat-packing industry. Words like *venal, slimy*, and *dysfunctional* are sprinkled throughout his book. Both authors have a long list of complaints, but the heart of their critique can be summed up succinctly: Mutual fund companies put their own interests ahead of yours.

But there is hope. Swensen offers some sound, if slightly boring, advice on how to use mutual funds wisely. His suggestions include the following:

+ Go with index funds. This is the hardest advice to swallow. It seems almost un-American to accept the notion that you won't be able to beat market benchmarks. Who wants to admit he is just average? But the hard, cold facts are that only a small percentage of actively managed funds beat index funds in the long run. In a study cited by Swensen, only twenty-two percent of funds beat the Vanguard 500 Index Fund over a twenty-year period. "Almost everyone believes he is going to be in those funds that outperform. In Lake Wobegon, all the children are above average. In the stock market, not everyone is so lucky.

73

* Pick funds with low fees that do only a limited amount of trading. Like Wal-Mart shoppers, investors should seek out everyday low prices, Again, index funds fit the bill. They have low fees and no managers, which means no one is buying and selling stocks, a process that can create tax liabilities. Swensen is a big fan of the Vanguard index funds, in large measure because Vanguard is a not-for-profit organization. You would think he, not Bogle, was the founder of Vanguard. In fact, a number of fund companies offer index funds that provide the same benefits as the Vanguard funds.

* Swensen's advice is far from sexy. It won't produce the astonishing returns he has generated at Yale. But his suggestions are smart and sensible. Most of us would do well to buy in. (Charles Stein, "Like Them or Not, We Need Mutual Funds," *Boston Sunday Globe*, October 9, 2005)

Beating the market means receiving a return on your Investment that is higher than the return on the indexes that we recommend in this book. Some of the wealthiest and smartest people in the world invested their fortunes with Bernie Madoff because he had the reputation of consistently beating the market. Guess what they learned? No one, I repeat no one, consistently outperforms the market as represented by the indexes. All of the Madoff investors who lost billions and billions of dollars wish they simply had invested in index funds rather than believing that there was any person or system that could outperform the market.

Dr. Paul Samuelson, Nobel Prize winning professor at M.I.T., capsulized the significance of this simple investment strategy when he said "The creation of the first index fund by John Bogle was the equivalent of the invention of the wheel and the alphabet."

I recently read *The Investment Answer* by Daniel Goldie and Gordon Murray. The book is noteworthy to me for how it came into being and how it confirms our own investment philosophy at Pearson Financial Services. In 2010, Gordon was diagnosed with an inoperable brain tumor and given six months to live. He decided to devote the last remaining days of his life to write a book to help investors benefit from what he learned as an executive at the highest levels of three of Wall Street's biggest firms. Interviewed by *The New York Times* before he died at age sixty, Gordon said about the book, "to have a purpose and a mission for me has been really special. It probably has added days to my life." Because of these circumstances, his exposé of Wall Street cannot be questioned. *The New York Times* also reported on November 27, 2010, "But the mere fact that Mr. Murray felt compelled to write it is itself a remarkable story of an almost willful ignorance of the futility of active money management." Mr. Murray now stands as one of the highest ranking Wall Street veterans to rail against the exorbitant fees and expenses charged by actively managed mutual funds and Wall Street stock brokerage firms.

Gordon's book explains that the best performance historically is a result of the lowest costs, not the "genius" of the active managers. He recommended that you simply use exchange traded index funds that cost five times less than the average cost of actively managed funds.

In a personal note at the end of Gordon's book he wrote he was "even luckier to have had the opportunity to give something back. For decades, we have watched much of the traditional financial services industry (which includes money managers, the mainstream financial media, as well as Wall Street brokers) take advantage of innocent, hard-working investors' lack of financial expertise and their behavioral tendencies. Deep down inside I knew there was a better way to invest. THIS IS IT."

This book is a must read. The first printing sold out immediately in 2010 and another printing of 150,000 copies has since been released in early 2011. The book is a quick read, absorbingly simple, seventy pages long, and I wish I had written it myself. To Gordon, active management is a case of paying someone else to gamble with your money with the same probability of success as flipping a coin. His mantra is our mantra: "A penny saved is a penny earned."

## Asset Allocation

According to investment experts, the choice about how to spread the money over those asset classes is the most significant factor in determining your portfolio's volatility.[3] It breaks down as follows:

+ Asset allocation: 91.5 percent
+ Security selection: 4.6 percent
+ Market timing: 1.8 percent
+ Other: 2.1 percent

---

[3] Gary P. Brinson. Brian D. Singer, and Gilbert P. Beebower, "Detriments of Portfolio Performance II," *Financial Analysts Journal* (May/June 1991).

In other words, who picks the stocks (security selection) and trying to get into the market during the lows and sell during the highs (market timing) have relatively insignificant impact on your returns or your risk—together, they amount to only 6.4 percent, which doesn't come close to touching the 91.5 percent contributed by asset allocation. And asset allocation is the key to modern portfolio theory.

An excellent asset allocation for dynasty trusts is to put approximately half your assets in individual Treasuries. Stocks should make up most of the other half, leaving some room for alternative investments, such as real estate investment trusts. Diversifying the riskiest half is the most difficult aspect, but we're fortunate to have the Nobel Prize–winning theory as our guide.

## One-half in Treasuries

About half of the trust value should be invested in a ladder of Treasuries to produce the maximum income and to reduce volatility. A one- to ten-year maturity should be selected to maximize the income. An equal amount of money is invested in each of the ten maturities, so every year, bonds will come due and be available to buy a ten-year bond. As a result, as interest rates go up, there will always be money coming due to invest at a higher rate.

**Tax-Sensitive Investing.** In chapter 4, you saw taxes' severe drag on investment return. Here is an example: An investor holding a portfolio over the last twenty years, with a beginning balance of one hundred thousand dollars, would have lost almost fifty percent of the value accumulated over time to taxes, which is likely to have disappointed any investor targeting a $1.3 million objective.

## TAXES HAVE BEEN A DRAG ON INVESTMENT RETURNS

*Growth of $100,000 (1977–1997)*

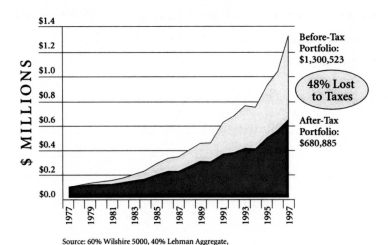

Source: 60% Wilshire 5000, 40% Lehman Aggregate,
50% Capital Gains Realization Rate, Highest Historical Tax Rates

This example represents a typical allocation of sixty percent to U.S. equity, and forty percent to U.S. fixed income, which is characteristic of the allocation of many tax-insensitive balanced funds. This chapter outlines the alternative: *a tax-sensitive, exchange-traded, index portfolio.*

# One-half in Stocks

Many studies point out that past performance is not a reliable indicator of future results. Then how will your family direct financial advisors to invest the stock portions of our trusts?

First, you want the portfolio to mimic the capitalization of the entire U.S. stock market. In general terms, that is about ninety percent in large company stocks and ten percent in small stocks today. Then we want about half to be growth stocks and half to be value stocks ("fallen stars").

Today, more than ever, some of the stock allocation should be in international stocks. The Euro countries, for instance, have more people combined than the U.S. They are educated, developed countries and will certainly compete with us to supply the needs of a world that will grow. China is legislating away from the communist system and moving to the free market system. The stock indexes of foreign stocks as measured by the unmanaged MSCI (Morgan Stanley Capital International) Country Index shows that the U.S. has not been the top performer in any of the last ten years. Names like New Zealand, Switzerland, Finland, Portugal, Spain, and Hong Kong have topped the charts.

Using the total U.S. stock market index fund from Vanguard, you can acquire over 3,000 stocks with an expense ratio of only .06 percent a year, and the modern portfolio solution for U.S. stocks is achieved.

But what about the rest of the world? About fifty percent of the world stock market value is outside the U.S. Certainly

China and India will develop into strong competition in the world economy. The world population will increase by fifty percent sometime in the second half of the century. Remember the Nobel Prize-winning economists, Sharpe and Markowitz, the founding fathers of modern portfolio theory? Markowitz said reducing volatility enhances the return, and Sharpe said owning all the stocks through an index outperforms buying and selling on average. So we add the "rest of the world" index to further reduce volatility leading to higher returns.

One academic study showed that during the thirty-three-year period from 1970 to 2003, a mix with seventy percent in the U.S. index and thirty percent in the foreign index would have produced a higher rate of return with less risk (volatility).

Thirty years ago, the United States produced seventy percent of the world domestic product. Today, we produce only fifty percent, and in our lifetimes our share will probably drop to thirty percent, more or less. So there it is: a simple solution for your stock portfolio, two index funds (seventy percent U.S. and fifty percent foreign) with over four thousand stocks. If 1990 was the birth of modern portfolio theory, then the last twenty years have only confirmed the academics' research.

To give more weight to the decision to allocate fifty to sixty percent of a lifetime income portfolio to stock, consider the following information from *Pension and Investments,* which appeared in its January 23, 2006 edition:

IBM has 58 percent of its pension in stocks, General Electric has 63 percent of its pension in stocks, Boeing has 59.5 percent, Verizon has 64 percent, AT&T has 56 percent, United Technologies has 70 percent, Daimler Chrysler 60.5 percent, and Bank of America 75 percent in stocks. Certainly the best and brightest are advising these pensions and you can be assured that modern portfolio theory provides the core structure for the stock allocation.

So, the father of modern portfolio theory advises us to diversify by buying everything using index funds to reduce volatility and increase the return. Indexing reduces the costs of diversifying by cutting out layers of fees, expenses, and taxes. Wall Street does not put your interests ahead of theirs. In 2005, which wasn't a great year for stocks, Wall Street paid bonuses of $21.5 billion to its senior executives. The chief executive of Merrill Lynch alone received a bonus of $14.1 million. These bonuses are a result of increased revenues from investors like you.

Diversification doesn't mean your index funds don't have risk, but that risk is less than owning a few stocks. For instance, over the last five years ending 31 December 2005, blue chip stocks like GE, Merck, GM, Pfizer, AT&T, AIG, Verizon, Coca-Cola, Eli Lilly, Intel, JP Morgan Chase, Wal-Mart, Disney, and Honeywell have all underperformed the unmanaged U.S. stock market index. Looking back at history, there is a fifty percent chance that any single stock in the S&P500 index will underperform the index itself by more than twenty percent over five years.

In summary then, modern portfolio theory is the overwhelming choice of many respected academics, economists, and investors. It's simple to build a core, stock portfolio solution around this Nobel Prize-winning theory using three low-cost, exchange-traded index funds.

## More on Costs

On July 9, 2007 *Investment News* reported that portfolio trading costs can be an even bigger drag on mutual fund performance than the expense ratio. A study conducted by Boston College together with Virginia Tech and University of Virginia of 1,706 funds for the ten year period between 1995 and 2005 determined that the funds spent 1.4 percent a year on trading costs compared with the 1.21 percent they spent on their expense ratio. Combined, you lose, on average, over 2.6 percent a year. If you are lucky enough to earn 10 percent a year, are you willing to pay Wall Street 26 percent of your earnings?

The following list of distinguished authors, including Nobel Prize winners, have written books supporting the low-cost, simple, index strategy that we recommend for the stock allocation in your Dynasty Trusts. They are: Burton Malkiel, John Bogle, William Bernstein, Larry Swedroe, Richard Ferri, David Swensen, Harry Markowitz, Gordon Murray, William Sharpe, Russell Wild, Craig Baird, Mike Piper, Dale Maley, Paul Samuelson, Peter Bernstein and Kenneth French.

Shortly after winning the Nobel Prize in Economics, William Sharpe wrote a watershed article in the *Financial*

*Analysts Journal* (January 1991). In two easy-to-understand pages he summarized the performance advantage of passive index investing. Essentially all the active managers combined own all the stocks. When one sells, another buys the same stock. However, because active managers have expenses, they underperform the index that also holds all the stocks. Index funds on average cost five times less than the average for actively managed mutual funds.

# Why "Balance" Your Portfolio This Way?

A balanced portfolio will provide a lifetime of income and the liquidity for unpredictable expenses like health care. Fixed, guaranteed investments like treasury bills need to be a part of the portfolio. Learn what you don't know and then apply what you learn about fixed income. There is no better source for learning than the 2005 book *Unconventional Success* by David Swensen, America's premier investor and manager of the $20 billion Yale Endowment. On page 104 of the book, Swensen has this to say about corporate bonds:

> Sensible investors avoid corporate debt, because credit risk and callability undermine the ability for fixed-income holdings to provide portfolio protection in times of financial or economic disruption. U.S. government bonds provide a superior alternative.

On page 110, he gives us the following observations on high yield bonds:

> The factors that promise incremental yield-credit risk, illiquidity, and callability work against junk-bond owners in times of crisis,

undermining the ability of junk bonds (high yield bonds) to provide portfolio protection.

Compared to treasuries, he said that "junk bond investors took greater risk for less return." What about municipal bonds? On page 117 of Swensen's book, he says, "Issues related to tax-rate uncertainty credit risk, call optionality, and trading costs combine to diminish in dramatic fashion the utility of tax-exempt bonds." Once again, he recommends the benefit of "non-callable, default-free U.S. Treasury Securities" for certain portfolio protection.

Therefore, a balanced portfolio designed to provide a lifetime of income protection from inflation and liquidity would include treasuries. For instance, when stock markets crash or correct, the treasuries provide the liquidity and reduce the overall risk (volatility) of the portfolio. Remember the Nobel Prize-winning theory: portfolios with "lower volatility will have the greatest compound rate of return over time."

How simple is this portfolio? It includes two or three index funds and two types of treasuries. The total internal cost of the portfolio is less than 0.2 percent per year. This portfolio did better in the past and will probably do better in the future for one obvious reason: it costs less. It sounds too good to be true, doesn't it? The best performing portfolio could have the least amount of risk (volatility), the lowest cost, and as few as four moving parts. If you don't believe it, just ask Warren Buffet, Professor Sharpe, or David Swensen.

# Bonds

When rates rise, bond values fall and the income that funds pay rises. If you don't sell the bond fund, your income will not be affected adversely, and eventually the interest rate cycle will reverse itself and bond prices will rise, increasing bond values and slowly reducing the income. On average, these cycles last about five years.

Another alternative is to buy the U.S. government bond itself. In this cycle we feel that rising stocks values will drive the total return of the portfolio but eventually the next recession will arrive and stock prices will fall. When that happens, historically, government bonds go up, reducing the overall volatility of the portfolio. The following information outlines a strategy that has helped many clients through the cycles of boom and bust, growth and recession, rising and falling interest rates.

## *Key characteristics of bonds*

**Average quality:** Independent bond-rating agencies, such as Standard & Poor's and Moody's Investors Service, evaluate the ability of taxable bond issuers to repay loans. These agencies assign credit rating ranging from Aaa or AAA (highest quality) to C or D (lowest quality).

**Average effective maturity:** The average length of time before bonds in a fund reach maturity and are repaid is known as the fund's average maturity. The average effective maturity affects a fund's yield as well as the level of risk to investors' principal. In general, the longer the average effective maturity, the more a fund's share price will fluctuate in response to changes in interest rates. A fund with an average effective maturity of one to five years is considered a short-term bond fund; one with a maturity of five to ten years, an intermediate-term bond fund; and one with a maturity of more than ten years, a long-term bond fund.

**Average duration:** This measurement can be used to estimate how much a bond fund's share price may rise or fall in response to a change in interest rates. Bond funds with long average durations (more than seven years) are likely to have negative returns during years when interest rates rise significantly. Bond funds with average durations of less than three years have rarely had negative calendar-years returns. Past performance, of course, is no guarantee of future returns.

# The U.S. Government Bond Strategy

The face value of a bond is the amount of money the investor will get back at maturity. The price of the bond fluctuates in value until it matures. When a bond sells for more than its face value it is at a premium, and when its price is below its face value, it is selling at a discount. The coupon is the interest that will be paid monthly or semi-annually and is a fixed percentage of the face value of the bond. Government bonds are the safest bonds.

The U.S. government bond is a direct obligation, and since the government can literally print money to pay back investors at maturity, it is generally considered a risk-free asset. However, as interest rates rise, the price of a bond falls so a sale of the bond before maturity could result in a loss. To avoid any loss of principal, you simply hold it until it matures and continue to collect the fixed interest payment, which is also guaranteed by the U.S. Government. When you invest in a government bond, it is very important to know what the yield to maturity is so there is no doubt about what you will receive in interest and ultimately in principal at maturity. The Government National Mortgage Association (GNMA), also known as a "Ginnie Mae", is a U.S. government-owned corporation. They are the only mortgage-backed securities guaranteed by the United States government. GNMA securities have the same credit rating as the government of the United States. The interest payments and the return of principal at maturity are guaranteed by the full faith and credit of the U.S. government.

The Ginnie Mae has no relationship at all to Fannie Maes or Freddie Macs which were stockholder corporations traded on the New York Stock Exchange and had absolutely no guarantee of principal or interest from the government and were part of the 2008 government bailout.

The U.S. government created the GNMA in 1968 to promote home ownership within the Department of Housing and Urban Development. Ginnie Mae buys home mortgages originated under programs run by the Federal Housing

Administration, the Veterans Administration and the Rural Housing Service. It then pools mortgages with similar characteristics and issues securities backed by the payments on the loans and guaranteed by the U.S. government at maturity. Since inception the GNMA has issued more than $2.1 trillion with about $500 billion currently outstanding.

# Bond Ladder

Successful investors have used the bond ladder strategy to reduce the interest rate risk of bonds. It is a portfolio that has different maturities. A GNMA Government bond has guaranteed principal payments every month spread out over the "average life" of the bond. If interest rates go up, you will receive principal each month to reinvest in bonds paying a higher rate, increasing the overall yield to maturity. If interest rates fall, all of the bond that doesn't mature each month continues to earn the higher rate which also protect the overall yield of the bond ladder. In other words, it is a strategy that can add value no matter which way rates move.

Each year the guaranteed principal of the maturing treasury is realized.

# Conclusion Recap:

- The Ginnie Mae interest and principal payments at maturity are guaranteed by the U.S. government.

- The key reason to invest in a GNMA is to maximize income and safety.

- The GNMA should be considered an intermediate term, fixed income investment.

- Government bonds are the safest bonds.

- A bond "ladder" can minimize the effect of rising or falling interest rates.

- The guaranteed liquidity of the GNMA is limited to the principal payments and interest payments each month during the "life" of the GNMA.

- The price, if you sell a GNMA before the maturity payments, fluctuates in value.

- The Ginnie Mae has no relation to the Fannie Mae of Freddie Mac corporations.

## Rebalancing the Portfolio

Rebalancing the portfolio ensures continued proper allocation to each asset class (bonds, large stocks, small stocks, and non-U.S. stocks) in the portfolio, while adding the benefit of a built-in "sell high, buy low" strategy.

Without rebalancing, the mix of assets in the portfolio may become skewed from the original plan. This will happen over time as different asset classes increase or decrease in value with shifting market conditions, and can lead to unplanned over- or under-exposure to certain asset classes.

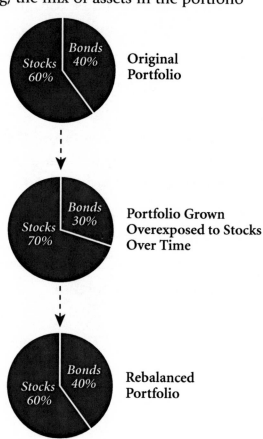

Original Portfolio

Portfolio Grown Overexposed to Stocks Over Time

Rebalanced Portfolio

The following chart illustrates how the trust should be diversified in the beginning. Rebalancing would mean returning the values back to this allocation.

# DIVERSIFYING A $1 MILLION INVESTMENT

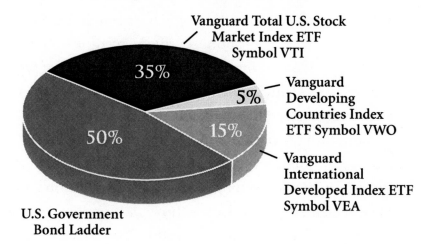

Vanguard Total U.S. Stock Market Index ETF Symbol VTI

Vanguard Developing Countries Index ETF Symbol VWO

Vanguard International Developed Index ETF Symbol VEA

U.S. Government Bond Ladder

## Applying Modern Portfolio Theory To Indexing

Modern portfolio theory can be followed with alternative investments. Indexing, for instance, is growing in popularity as more studies suggest the low costs of index funds mean higher returns for the investor. There are too many index funds for the average investor to pick from, so rely on your advisor to pick the best ones for your trust. For example, the

Vanguard U.S. Total Market Index exchange traded fund is simply a basket of stocks that closely track the composition of the total market index. This basket holds thousands of stocks, and its composition meets your advisor's criteria for diversification and asset allocation, just like the stock portfolio discussed earlier. The exchange traded fund works like a stock: It can be bought and sold through any brokerage account throughout the trading day. It is a uniquely efficient investment that costs about seventy percent less than most funds. Professional investors argue the question of which way is best: *actively* buying and selling to try and beat the market, or *passively* buying the market using index funds.

One thing is certain: Most active managers fail to outperform their respective index. The main reasons are the cost of buying and selling stocks and the additional expense of management. As you know now, past performance is no guarantee of future results. Your financial advisor should continue to monitor the performance of the stock managers. The best way to judge how well your money managers are doing is to compare their total return to the U.S. Total Market Index each year. If, over a period of three years or more, the active managers are under-performing the index fund, you should look at making some changes. The best active managers will modify their portfolios over time to include indexing as a core holding.

Modern Portfolio Theory uses historic returns to optimize the probability of higher future returns with less volatility or risk. Using that premise, our recommended asset allocation would have fifty percent in the treasury bond ladder and fifty percent in stock index funds. Seventy percent of the stock allocation would be the Total U.S. Stock Market Index, twenty-five percent would be in the developed Foreign Index and five percent would be in the developing countries index that includes Brazil, Russia, India and China (the "BRIC" countries). Combined there would be more than five thousand stocks in these three index funds.

Some people have a very low tolerance for volatility. If you will sell when stocks are down, it might make more sense to have an allocation with about thirty percent in stocks and seventy percent in bonds. You also might reduce the stock allocation when the price earnings ratio is clearly signaling stocks are overpriced. But don't forget that an allocation of at least thirty percent to stocks may be needed to keep up with inflation over a lifetime that may be longer than you ever imagined.

From 1926 through 2012, stocks (as measured by the S&P500 index) have averaged over 9.8 percent. This period includes the Great Depression and every major crash since then. Over the same period, intermediate term treasury bonds have earned about 5 percent and "risk less" treasury bills have averaged 3.8 percent. Inflation averaged 3 percent. Why do we think this history is so important? Ben Bernanke and his predecessors were hired for the most important financial position in the world to apply what they learned studying economic history. Like Ben, those of us who use Modern Portfolio Theory use history to advise our clients as to the probability of future outcomes. There is absolutely no academic research to support a better strategy. Today as we all worry about the unprecedented deficit, the uncertainty in the Middle East and the politicians in Washington, I am comforted by history and something Winston Churchill said: "America, after exhausting every other alternative, will do the right thing."

## Simplifying Matters

Clearly, this chapter offers only an overview of investing for the dynasty trust. For your trust to be skillfully administered, you need to ensure you put the investment management in capable hands. Although it's important that you and your family understand at least the basics of investing and pay regular attention to how your trust is managed, you do not have to become an authority on investments just so your trust can be handled properly. On the contrary; if you select tested, trusted team members—a core group of financial professionals, a reputable trustee, and effective money managers—then all you must do is reap the benefit of their expertise and attend to their performance. By structuring your trust as a dynasty trust, you will set up a series of checks and balances that will keep you up to date on your trust's appreciation and also alert you if anything needs to be changed.

# 7

# Deal With the Future: Help Your Family Cope

Once you've made the decision to establish a dynasty trust, found the best people to put it together and administer it for you, and signed on the dotted line, you have an entirely new responsibility: guiding your children to become effective, informed guardians of the gift they will one day receive. It's one thing to create a trust and entirely another to reap its benefits with wisdom.

When your trust is finalized, everything looks great on paper. But at this point, it's mostly all still theory, and any potential problems are yet to be seen. No matter how prepared you are, your dynasty trust can't handle every possible eventuality on its own. To work for you, it requires that your family attend to four key areas: the family's own decision-making process, the independent trustee's actions, the family financial advisor's services, and the custodian's services and fees. The main reason you established this trust in the first place was to leave assets to your family in the best possible way. Because things can and will change, the family has complete control and can change any of these four elements to their best advantage at any time.

*The Custodian.* The custodian's sole responsibility is to "hold" your assets, just as your bank has custody of your checking account funds or your mutual fund manager has custody of your investment funds. In a well-planned trust, the trustee is also the custodian, but of course this is not the only possible way to assign responsibilities. It may be that you decide to have a separate trustee and custodian. In this case, you'll need to keep an eye on both, and specifically watch for any changes in the custodian's fees or services. If fees increase or services decrease, the family should explore alternatives. It's a simple thing to change custodians if need be, and there is no fee, penalty, or tax cost to transfer the assets from one custodian to another.

*Financial Advisor.* Before anything else, ensure your advisor is fee based. Then the advisor's interest and the family's coincide, and everyone will want the highest rate of return and the lowest volatility (risk). (Note: Checks should never be made out directly to any advisor, only to custodian.) The advisor will not have discretion to buy or sell anything without family permission. The advisor will offer guidance on the options and recommend the ones he or she feels are best, but the family will ultimately decide. Likewise, if major changes are suggested, such as switching the trustee, the beneficiaries are obliged to carefully examine and consider the rationale and then make the decision.

*Independent Trustee.* The trustee's responsibilities include administration, tax returns, and protecting the assets from liability including divorce, automobile liability, bankruptcy, and other predators. The independent trustee role and fee are based on the premise the independent trustee is part of the team along with the investment advisor—but the family should always make the ultimate decisions. Your trust agreement should detail these responsibilities, as well as the checks and balances built in to minimize any trouble with an independent trustee. In most cases, family members will act as trustees.

Care must be taken to monitor the investments at least once a month. (Your family can set up direct, secure, Internet access available through your trustee.) Any significant change in value in the trust assets should prompt a call to the financial advisor, who will suggest any course of action he or she sees necessary.

*Family Decisions.* One almost entirely avoidable problem could arise if your heirs use their power to take everything out of the trust, thereby ending its usefulness. If it is removed, the money would no longer be protected from liability or tax. By now, my opinion about this should be crystal clear: Taking assets out of the dynasty trust would be an uninformed mistake. Seventy percent of everyone in America wants financial help, and the family bank can provide that help—as long as the assets remain in trust.

Remember, your heirs can borrow from the trust, giving them virtually the same access as a withdrawal, while maintaining the maximum asset protection and tax benefits available. You can help your family understand this by giving them a copy of this book and by informing and including them as you create your trust. Be sure to use the services of the family office, too, to help educate your children and accustom them to the rewards of expert counsel on all financial matters, from home mortgages to car purchases to IRA investing. At minimum, be sure your children understand how the dynasty trust provides them with the following:

* Unequalled protection of the assets from liability
* Access to tax-free and interest-free loans
* Personalized financial advice and service
* A customized portfolio
* Highly diversified, global asset allocation
* Lower costs because of institutional pricing
* Risk reduction through automatic rebalancing
* A team of specialist money managers
* Continuous manager monitoring
* Excellent reporting
* Tax return preparation and active tax management
* Help to secure their family's financial future

Providing and encouraging this education is probably the single most important thing you can do to assure that the dynasty trust you establish will live forever. In this country, it's all too common for family wealth to dwindle and disappear within just three generations. But you can be the exception. By offering your children the grand gift not only of tax avoidance and asset protection through the dynasty trust, but also the wisdom to become caretakers of and contributors to a family legacy, you provide them with so many other incredible, intangible gifts they could get from no one else. Why leave your assets any other way?

Help your family cope after you are gone by establishing relationships with trusted advisors now. Simplify the investment process so it will be easy for your family to follow a plan that you design based on your lifetime of experience. The goal is simple: security. True wealth in the end is nothing more than having enough.

# *Appendix: You Have Our Trust*

Now that you know all of the important, general information about the dynasty trust—the far-reaching benefits to your family and the approximate costs for set-up and administration—it's time for you to become acquainted with the specifics of my particular model. My trust design comes from more than thirty years of personal and business experience with thousands of trusts and many millions of dollars. I have consulted with two of the biggest trust companies in the nation and experienced, firsthand, both the benefits of a properly executed trust and the problems associated with improper, inflexible estate planning. I'm one of the most experienced Certified Financial Planner™ professionals in the country, and few (if any) have more hands-on, direct involvement with more clients and their trusts over the last three decades. Consequently, I offer the following details of my trust design as a standard bearer for you as you proceed with your own estate planning. It is simple, and you can easily learn what you need to customize your own legacy plan in collaboration with your chosen estate planning professionals.

The following should serve as a review of the recommendations you've received so far, while amplifying them with details of a specific trust. In this example, we employ all that you've learned to this point.

* We use a trust when needed to minimize state taxes, maximize privacy, and protect the assets from creditors for future generations without transfer (estate/death) taxes—forever.

* We put control in the hands of the inheritors and provide for two exit strategies whereby the heirs can draw the entire trust principal if they feel it is to their benefit.

* We remove conflicts of interest and hidden agendas from the service providers.

* The trust will hold investments in bonds, stocks, mutual funds, treasuries, and real estate. It will be the beneficiary of any life insurance held at the time of death.

* The trust may be funded at any time to leverage the tax savings. A family limited partnership may be added to the trust to increase the amount protected in the trust.

* The family bank is the source of comprehensive financial services; however, beneficiaries will be coached never to delegate away the control. They must become and remain involved and informed.

+ A team of tested, trusted advisors will administer the trust. Beneficiaries have the ability to hire and fire them as needed in the future.
+ Total costs should not exceed those of a typical mutual fund. The trust is designed to be a profit center, customized for flexibility and personal attention.

Below I use my own family's dynasty trust as an example. This should give you my unadulterated view of the optimal way to set up a trust (who else, if not my own children, would get my best advice?), and it will also answer several questions you might ask yourself if it were your trust: If something happened today, how would my family bank's financial advisors invest the money? Who is the trustee? Why would we place our trust in this team? How am I able to access all of these services for such a low cost? And, most important, how can future generations stay informed on all key financial matters?

Our real estate will be held in trust. Because there is no management involved, all investment advisory fees are waived. The family continues to have the option of selling the property or removing it from the trust. My personal plan will direct the family to sell the real estate and invest the proceeds in the trust.

Currently, our dynasty trust will be funded when we die. At that time, my children will act as their own trustees. Once again, the family has complete control and flexibility.

*Our Financial Advisors.* My own advisory practice, which I founded more than thirty years ago, will act as the initial financial advisor for my family. It will provide liaison services and communication to all beneficiaries no matter where they reside—anywhere in the world. It will partner with the family to provide the following trust services:

+ Managing wealth with sophisticated, tax-sensitive investment management strategies
+ Maintaining custody of all securities
+ Processing and confirming all purchases and sales of securities
+ Collecting dividends and interest
+ Investing daily cash balances in a money market fund
+ Paying beneficiaries exactly as required by the trust agreement
+ Providing income checks or wired direct deposits to beneficiaries as they request
+ Sending monthly and annual statements of holdings and transactions and performance summaries of trust investments

Though the totality of these services may strike you as complicated, they actually simplify things for the family. Yes, they require expertise to accomplish, but not from the family. The objective is to put a team in place we can trust to protect, invest, and distribute our wealth efficiently. We want to free our children from these financial necessities so they can focus on their own families and careers.

*Estate Settlement.* Upon our death, the attorney who drew up the trust will work with my firm to settle our estate and place the assets in the trust. The settlement cost will be an hourly fee—not a percentage of the estate.

*Portfolio Management.* Half of our portfolio will be invested in stocks, and the other half will be invested in treasuries. The team will provide everything the beneficiaries need to fully understand the comprehensive, consolidated statement. The reporting tracks the activity of the investments and provides a clear picture of how assets are invested. The format is easy to read and reduces much of the confusion associated with traditional statements. A quarterly performance report provides an in-depth analysis of the portfolio's return and allows the beneficiaries to measure the manager's performance against relevant market indexes.

At year-end, the family will receive an organized tax report that summarizes year-to-date totals for both short- and long-term capital gains and dividends. Most important, the financial advisory team is there to provide the highest level of personalized service anywhere in the country, whether it's reviewing the status of the account or consulting on any other financial matter of concern family members may have.

*Exit Strategies.* My family will have complete discretion over the trust. They will retain the ability to replace trustees, advisors, and agents any time. They will have the right to borrow up to one hundred percent of the trust assets, interest-free, as long as the law allows. They could also close the trust, removing all the assets. (In my opinion, which you

105

certainly have gathered by now, borrowing is superior to closing the trust, which eliminates all of the tax and asset-protection benefits for which we created it in the first place. But the family will have the right to do as it sees fit.)

***Putting It All Together.*** In summary, my family will select the initial financial advisor, and the trustee will provide custody and accounting. The team will screen investment alternatives, acting as a gatekeeper for family assets. It will provide caring, skillful, personalized service to all family members, allowing them the peace of mind that comes with confidence.

In today's complex world of investment opportunity, even the most knowledgeable people find it difficult to develop and implement a well-structured investment plan on their own. That's why we've structured this team as we have. With all these pieces in place, my family's trust assets are fully invested with a world-class team of financial specialists. The family financial advisor checks on the trustee. In turn, the trustee monitors the managers, and the beneficiaries gain the advantages from objective supervision at every level of the investment process. I believe this dynasty trust plan will provide my children and grandchildren with experienced investment, legal, and accounting professionals. Experts committed to providing the highest level of personal service over the long term, combined with a time-tested strategy implemented by trusted advisors to preserve and grow our assets, is a wonderful legacy in itself.

This book, then, is about two subjects; establishing the best estate plan and developing the optimal investment strategy.

## I. The Dynasty Estate Plan

The idea is to simply protect inheritances from creditors, from divorcing spouses, from automobile liability and professional liability, as well as state and federal death taxes as long as the family needs and wants that protection. The Dynasty Trust can offer these benefits for many generations.

## II. Passive Investment and Modern Portfolio Theory

On the investment side, we outlined a strategy that I call the four T's: Tested, Trusted, Transparent and Total cost.

**Tested:** The index performance is known and recorded for over eighty years.

**Trusted**: The proponents of this strategy are respected academics.

**Transparent**: The more than five thousand stocks in these indexes are listed daily, open to public scrutiny.

**Total Costs:** The lower the costs, the more you earn. "A penny saved is a penny earned."

Seek advice, study the options you have, make the best decisions you can. Then enjoy the time you have left.

# ABOUT THE AUTHOR

S ETH M. PEARSON, CFP is one of the country's most experienced financial planners. He advises clients with assets totaling more than a quarter of a billion dollars.

With a perspective gained from more than thirty years of helping thousands of families make important financial decisions, he is uniquely qualified to act as a consumer advocate. His gift is using the education and experience he's gained both personally and as a financial professional to guide families through the many hidden agendas and conflicts of interest so prevalent in the financial and legal services industries today.

In addition to his career as a financial advisor, he has consulted with three of the largest financial institutions in the nation and lectured to more than eighteen thousand people on the science and art of financial planning. Seth lives with his wife, Penny, on Cape Cod, Massachusetts, and his three children and six grandchildren live nearby.

CPSIA information can be obtained at www.ICGtesting.com
Printed in the USA
BVOW081541300413

319429BV00001B/1/P